South to the Future

South to the Future

An American Region in the Twenty-first Century

EDITED BY FRED HOBSON

Mercer University Lamar Memorial Lectures No. 44

THE UNIVERSITY OF GEORGIA PRESS

Athens and London

Designed by Sandra Strother Hudson
Photograph on page iii by Valerie Fleming
Set in Adobe Garamond by BookComp, Inc.
Printed and bound by Thomson-Shore
The paper in this book meets the guidelines for permanence
and durability of the Committee on Production Guidelines
for Book Longevity of the Council on Library Resources.
Printed in the United States of America
06 05 04 03 02 C 5 4 3 2 1

Library of Congress Cataloging-in-Publication Data

South to the future : an American region in the twenty-first
century / edited by Fred Hobson.
        p. cm. — (Mercer University Lamar memorial lectures ;
no. 44)
Essays based on talks given at the Lamar 2000 Symposium, held
at Mercer University, Oct. 2000.
Includes bibliographical references.
ISBN 0-8203-2411-6 (alk. paper)
1. Pluralism (Social sciences)—Southern States—Congresses.
2. Regionalism—Southern States—Congresses. 3. American
literature—Southern States—Congresses. 4. Southern States—
Civilization—Congresses. 5. Southern States—Social conditions—
Congresses. 6. Southern states—Civilization—Forecasting—
Congresses. I. Title. II. Series.
F209.5 .S66 2002
975—dc21   2001052259

British Library Cataloging-in-Publication Data available

Contents

Foreword

In a Lamar Lectures committee meeting in 1996, Henry Warnock of Mercer University's Department of History suggested that the committee try to produce something special for the year 2000. Instead of our traditional format of having one lecturer deliver three lectures over the course of two days, we asked four scholarly observers of southern history, literature, and culture to deliver one short lecture each on the subject of the South and the twenty-first century and to join in a panel discussion after the lectures. For this year only, the name Lamar Lectures was changed to the Lamar 2000 Symposium.

With the help of many individuals and organizations, the symposium was held October 21. The committee welcomes this chance to thank those who helped make the 2000 symposium indeed extraordinary.

Committee member Fred Hobson advised us on our choices of lecturers, edited the lectures, and wrote the introduction to this book. Kirby Godsey, the president of Mercer University, supported our effort from the beginning; Emily Myers, Vice President of Advancement, lent us her capable workers, Jennifer Barfield and Terri Newham, who were always diligent about supervision and detail. Bobbie Shipley, besides all her tasks as programs specialist in the Department of Interdisciplinary Studies, has been the rock the Lamar Lectures have leaned on for the last decade and was, as always, an important consultant. Hosts of cooks, servers, drivers, custodians, and sound technicians performed their jobs with care and punctuality.

We are grateful also to the former lecturers and their spouses who by attending made the occasion even more distinguished: Robert Brinkmeyer and his wife Debra Cohen, Trudier Harris, Samuel and Helen Hill, Fred Hobson, Lucinda and John MacKethan, and John and Dale Reed. Their assembly with the symposium's four lecturers generated an unprecedentedly high level of Lamar Lectures fellowship, and that alone justified the energy expended in bringing the symposium together.

Committee member Sarah Gardner, who became the committee's chairperson in 2001, moderated the panel discussion with her customary liveliness and comprehensive insight. Karen Orchard and the University of Georgia Press were typically superb in their management and production of this book.

Most of all the committee wishes to thank the lecturers, whose reflections on the South of the future you will read in the following pages. Each of them conquered the limitations we placed on their time at the lectern and gave interesting and, indeed, lively talks, and each of them contributed thoughtfully to the panel discussion. Finally, none of this would have been possible without the generosity of Eugenia Dorothy Blount Lamar, whose bequest to Mercer University almost half a century ago specified a series of lectures of "the very highest type of scholarship" that would "aid in the permanent preservation of the values of southern culture, history, and literature."

MICHAEL M. CASS

For the Lamar Memorial Lectures Committee

South to the Future

lying south of South. In fact, to that more encompassing South, the U.S. South is essentially *el norte*. All is relative, all depends on point of view, all the more so now that a significant portion of the population of that larger, deeper South has come north. The South is no longer even *perceived* as standing alone. It must be seen in the larger picture.[1]

This is only one of many ways in which the U.S. South is viewed differently as it enters a new millennium. Another is that, currently, much of the finest work on the South focuses not on its uniqueness but rather on its similarity to other regions and cultures. One might, for example, examine its parallels with certain European nations (with proud, defiant but defeated *parts* of those nations in particular); or one might, citing any number of historical and economic parallels, view the South as another postcolonial region; or one might see it in relation to racially charged and racially divided nations (for example, South Africa). All are profitable ways of approaching the southern regions of the United States. In many respects, of course, the historian C. Vann Woodward got there first. In his 1952 essay, "The Irony of Southern History," he quite rightly pointed out all that the U.S. South (but not—in those pre-Vietnam days—the rest of the United States) had in common with all "other people of the civilized world": defeat, poverty, failure, frustration, and "a knowledge that history has happened to our people in our part of the world." (Woodward was attributing these qualities to white southerners, but poverty, frustration, failure, and a *felt* knowledge of history also apply, even more strongly if for quite different reasons, to black southerners.) In any case, the uniqueness of the South *within* the United States—the Southern Agrarians notwithstanding—could always have been challenged on many fronts. Certain of the Agrarians and their apostles had affirmed that the southerner (by which they generally meant the white male southerner) viewed the world differently than did the representative American—that the southerner saw the world concretely, not abstractly; that the southerner had a stronger sense of place and a more abiding religious sense than the nonsoutherner; and so on. Perhaps in the ways Woodward suggested—ways connected with history and failure *within* history—the white southerner might indeed have viewed reality somewhat differently than, say, an Ohioan. But not in numerous other ways.

I would venture, for example, that an inhabitant of Vermont or rural Indiana (that is, any place that has a relatively homogeneous population and has been settled for at least a century and a half) has just as pronounced a sense of place—and, often, just as strong a religious sense—as an inhabitant of rural Georgia. As far as the alleged southern rage against abstraction is concerned, no Americans have relied more heavily on abstractions than white southerners. The emphasis on honor, chivalry, gyneolatry—not to mention race itself, and the segregation resulting from its distinctions—all rest on abstractions. The very act of describing the "representative" southerner was itself a prime act of abstracting.

But to return to my primary point: in so many ways accepted wisdom about the South—what it was and is and means—is changing radically because concepts of religion, place, race, culture, and community are being reevaluated. I take *culture* as an example and find it instructive that the term, used in its southern context, is now almost always plural, culture*s*. In 1934 the University of North Carolina Press published its monumental *Culture in the South;* now that same press publishes an enlightening (and entertaining) journal named *Southern Cultures*. The distinction is an important one. Once (if not altogether to W. T. Couch, editor of *Culture in the South,* certainly to H. L. Mencken and W. J. Cash) "culture" meant only *high* culture, that quality measured by libraries, museums, and symphonies. It was in that sense that the South was a Sahara. But at the very time Mencken and then Cash were pronouncing it so—when one considers culture in its totality, that is, as the expression of a people (or people*s*) demonstrated in storytelling, music, folk dance, and numerous other activities—it was far from a desert. When Mencken and Cash were writing, jazz and the blues, among other art forms, were flourishing, but neither man would have accepted such expression as culture.

One might similarly reevaluate that staple of southern literary discourse, *community*. To the Agrarians and to many of their followers, the traditional South had a stronger sense of community than other areas did, and that was altogether a good thing. Community meant people who knew each other, people united by shared values and a similar outlook, people blessed with a common sense of place—in short, what Henry Adams and T. S. Eliot might have called an organic society. That was fine in certain respects, but far from fine in others. The community that included could exclude as well. People in place often meant people in their *places*. A reconsideration of race, gender, and class—a consideration of hierarchy in all its forms—complicates the idea of community, the idea of an organic society of any sort. That, in fact, was always the case: a sense of harmony and "shared values" are just other ways of expressing what Cash, in *The Mind of the South*, called "the savage ideal"—that "ideal whereunder dissent and variety are completely suppressed and men become, in their attitudes, professions, and actions, virtual replicas of each other." To the outsider who ventures into such a community—or to the spiritual outsider within it—the world is not always kind.

Long-held assumptions about southern literature have been radically altered, of course, in part because the South itself has changed so radically. The reality—and, even more, the mythology—of the poor, failed, defeated, backward-looking South has long since been replaced by the mythology of what in the 1970s came to be called the Sun Belt—prosperous, optimistic, forward-looking, air-conditioned, self-congratulatory, and guilt-free. *Southern Living* replaced Erskine Caldwell—and Peachtree Street, Tobacco Road. That the new mythology is not altogether grounded in reality is hardly the point; not only for the southern scholar but also for the southern writer of fiction, the old assumptions about Dixie hardly suffice. Southern writers, at least white southern writers, went through a rather awkward period in the 1960s and 1970s; the shadow of Faulkner still loomed large, and works such as William Styron's *Confessions of Nat Turner* (1967) and Eudora Welty's *Losing Battles* (1970) belonged in many respects to an earlier tradition. Other writers then (and some since) embarked on a desperate attempt to find continued southern distinctiveness—and, in the process, created a fiction that often rested on a contrived southern self-consciousness, a sort of neo-local color, almost a parody of the original. Writing at the same time, Walker Percy was in many ways an effective transitional figure, linking the Old South (what else was William Alexander Percy?—or Aunt Emily in *The Moviegoer?*) and the most recent of many New Souths (suburbs, country clubs, a more flexible idea of place). Since the late 1960s—as a literary force—Percy has become a more important writer than Faulkner; witness Josephine Humphreys in *Dreams of Sleep*, Richard Ford in *The Sportswriter,* and several other contemporary novelists. But the revolution in southern thought and expression goes far beyond that: the southern drama has witnessed a radical shift even since Percy's work of the 1970s and 1980s. Not only, in that newest drama, do the actors, white and black, assume different roles (not to mention gender—most Huck Finns in contemporary southern fiction are female); in many cases the actors are not even the same—that is, no longer *just* black and white. Multiculturalism in the South is not just theory; it is fact. As Thadious Davis points out, Robert Olen Butler writes of Vietnamese in Louisiana, and Judith Ortiz Cofer writes of growing up Puerto Rican in Georgia. Other writers depict Latinos and Latinas in south Florida and Hispanic farm workers and chicken-plant employees in piedmont North Carolina. Matters of class are perhaps even more complicated than matters of race and ethnicity. Granted, issues of class have always been important in southern life. From William Byrd through the Southwestern Humorists to Faulkner and Caldwell and beyond (not to mention historians and sociologists), poor white southerners have been depicted, dissected, and displayed—as well as lamented,

Williamson, in remarks during a panel discussion after his Lamar talk, is a case in point. "I didn't know southern history until I read Faulkner," he said, and neither did he really know the South, he would add, until he went in search of that other notable Mississippian, Elvis. A result of the former quest was Williamson's prize-winning *William Faulkner and Southern History* (1993), a result of the latter will be his forthcoming book, *The Feminine Elvis*. These two works take their places beside his classic study *The Crucible of Race* (1984). In his Lamar essay Williamson challenges still other historians to venture into southern letters and other aspects of southern culture(s). "If historians have been 'hobbled' in the past," he writes, "it is because we hobbled ourselves, fenced off certain areas and denied ourselves permission even to contemplate its terrain, much less trod that ground." Race is at the center of Williamson's discussion (as it has been at the center of so much of his finest work), or, more precisely, that treacherous intersection of race, class, and gender. "In America race touches everything," he asserts, and in fact all is inter-related: "The mainline southern mind long knew that if the blacks broke out, the women would break out too, and if the blacks and the women broke out, the rednecks would rise and all hell would break loose."

Wagner-Martin, in "The South as Universe," focuses more specifically on literature, and she brings to her discussion a deep knowledge of southern letters in relation to American letters in a broader sense. The author of biographies of Gertrude Stein, Ellen Glasgow, Sylvia Plath, and others, Wagner-Martin has also written and edited books on numerous other American authors, ranging from Hemingway and Faulkner to Denise Levertov and Joyce Carol Oates. That *oeuvre*, as well as her coeditorship of *The Oxford Companion to Women's Writing in the United States*, suggests the breadth of her vision, but in her Lamar essay she focuses on contemporary southern fiction. In that essay she is well grounded in what has gone before—she brings Poe, Mark Twain, and Margaret Mitchell into her discussion, as well as such traditional southern concerns as community, religion, racial conflict, and the relationship between humanity and nature—but what primarily interests her is the innovative use contemporary writers make of these traditional concerns. To her (as to the other essayists in this collection), "race" means more than the traditional black-white binary: as one example, in Charles Frazier's *Cold Mountain* (1997), since most of the white characters are hill people, "poor farmers and not slaveholders," Frazier "does not touch on any [traditional] racial issues. [*Cold Mountain*] instead posits the Native American, the Cherokee personified in the wise Swimmer and other characters, as the cultural 'other.'" In her discussions of Alice Walker, Barbara Kingsolver, and Cormac McCarthy, Wagner-Martin demonstrates the manner in which both race and place break down as southern imperatives. In McCarthy and Kingsolver in particular, "place" becomes "space," as "South" goes far beyond the borders of the old Dixie. Concluding with a discussion of contemporary southern women's fiction, Wagner-Martin insists that the "immediacy of modern life," as it is demonstrated in the fiction of Lee Smith, Jill McCorkle, and other writers, offers "universalizing themes that make these southern narratives stories of today's Everywoman."

In her essay, "Sashaying through the South," Thadious Davis is largely concerned with an even younger generation of southern, principally African American, writers. The author of numerous works, including the prize-winning *Nella Larsen: Novelist of the Harlem Renaissance*, Davis turns here to "what Shay Youngblood and youngsters are saying as twenty-first century southern writers." It is clear that Youngblood, born in 1959, and Randall Kenan, born in 1963, inhabit a world radically different not only from the writers of the Southern Renaissance (Faulkner, Warren, Wright, Welty) and their successors (Percy, Styron, Elizabeth Spencer, Margaret Walker) but also from *their* successors, writers such as Lee Smith, Josephine Humphreys, Barry Hannah, and Richard Ford who were born in the 1940s. One might, if one were into such labeling, call Youngblood and Kenan, as well as Donna Tartt, Mona Lisa Salloy, and others whom Davis brings into her discussion, the *fourth* generation of modern/postmodern southern literary expression: they were all born in the late 1950s or the 1960s—after *Brown v. Board of Education,* in some cases after even the 1960s heyday of the Civil Rights movement, thus after the death of the prevailing mythology (if not altogether the reality) of the poor, failed, defeated, tragic South. These writers "who will make the literature we may still call southern in the twenty-first century" are, in Davis's words, "diverse, sassy, and savvy." They "have come of age when they have the freedom to define themselves and their work in more than regional or racial terms. They may define their subject positions as multiply intersectional with gender and sexuality, religion and class, as significant as the markers of identity that would include race and region of birth or affiliation. In spatial terms, they also have a genuinely late-twentieth–early-twenty-first-century freedom of mobility. . . . They belong wherever they are." In the most stimulating—and entertaining—treatment of *fin de* (twentieth) *siècle* and early-twenty-first-century southern fiction one is likely to find, Davis considers such matters as "the collapsing of a distinction between the literary and the popular," the "humorously self-reflexive" nature of much twenty-first-century southern writing, the displacement of place in southern discourse (in which "Where are you from?" is as outmoded a question as "Who are your people?"), and—as do the other essayists here—the breakdown of the exclusively black-white polarity in race. Kenan, in particular, "produces a South and a southern past that has little to do with Faulkner's Yoknapatawpha or Gaines's Bayonne and everything to do with the kind of creation that marked those earlier fictionists."

If Davis's essay straddles that line between the twentieth and the twenty-first centuries, the piece by Edward Ayers is located altogether in the twenty-first. The author and editor of several books contemplating the southern past—including the much heralded *Promise of the New South: Life after Reconstruction* (1992)—here Ayers considers the future. I have spoken of the tendency of historians to become scholars of creative writing; Ayers does other historians one better and *becomes* a creative writer—of a sort. In "The Inevitable Future of the South"—a future Ayers says is anything but inevitable save in the mind of the hubristic sixteen-year-old narrator of his creation, telling his story in the year 2076—the historian joins Edward Bellamy, George Orwell, and other future-gazers, in Ayers's case describing a South of the late twenty-first century—which is to say, a society that occupies the land on which once rested a cultural and political entity known as the South. I will resist revealing the particulars of the society that Ayers's Scottish-Ghanian-Honduran-Korean-Cherokee schoolboy describes from his vantage point of 2076 (thirty-three years after the Great Consolidation, in which individual states ceded their power to a centralized authority based in Atlanta), except to say that, like all works projecting the future, this one is really at least as much about the present.

What all of these essays have in common is an excitement about the contemporary South—in whatever way one chooses to define it—and about southern change as the region enters the twenty-first century. It is not inappropriate that change should be the keynote of these lectures, as of so many other volumes in this series in recent years. The Lamar Lectures series itself has seen significant alterations since its beginnings—its very existence owing to the generous bequest of a Georgia woman, Dorothy Eugenia Blount Lamar, who was a former president of the United Daughters of the Confederacy, its first lecturer being the thoroughly unreconstructed Donald Davidson. One finds in the 2000 lectures, however, few "backward glances" and only a few reflections on the power of "the past in the present." Those phrases, of course, belong to (or have been employed to explain) the southern 1920s, a decade that, along with the 1960s, was the South's most revolutionary of the twentieth century. That earlier decade saw as well the beginning of what is generally called the Southern Literary Renaissance, although in fact what happened in the 1920s went far beyond literature, since that decade also saw the awakening of the southern critical spirit in a larger sense. What happened to southern writing in the 1920s and in the following decade served to disprove the assertion by the Agrarian Davidson that a condition of harmony between the author and his or her social and political environment provided the most conducive setting for the production of successful literature—and, conversely, that tension between a writer and his or her social environment leads to poor art. In fact, I would contend, the truth was—and is—precisely the opposite: the greatest literature is often a *product* of social and political tension, and the greatest writing has usually emerged during or just after periods of great tension and intellectual ferment: the English Renaissance; the American (which was in truth, the New England and New York) Renaissance of the 1830s and 1840s, a time characterized by the clashing of ways of life and freedom's ferment; and, yes, the Southern Renaissance of the 1920s and 1930s.

But, in truth, that period of the '20s and '30s, as well as that other charged southern decade, the 1960s, may pale in comparison with the present as a revolutionary time in the U.S. South—because, as I suggested earlier and as the essayists in this volume demonstrate, this time not only the stakes but also the very participants have changed. The issues now are more complex (quite literally, no longer black and white), the answers less morally certain, the tensions not even so easily defined. If one is looking for a revolutionary age in the U.S. South, it is upon us, and the essays in this volume wrestle mightily with its perils and its promise.

NOTE

1. What is called the South, even in its U.S. context, has always shifted, of course. In the nineteenth century, Maryland and even Delaware were usually included among the southern states; today, neither would claim much southern identity. Baltimore, which in the 1850s was very much a southern city, would hardly be seen as such now. Neither would

Eudora Welty once commented on what it was like for her to live and write in the same time and place with William Faulkner. It's like living next to a "mountain," she said. The same might be said of southern historians in relation to Vann Woodward. In Faulknerian terms, C. Vann Woodward is "the bear."

In his 1975 essay, Professor Woodward raised the question of why there was a Southern Renaissance, only to insist, amazingly, that we historians cannot answer that question. In the first place, he said, we don't have the instruments for the task. Typically, we deal with "groups rather than individuals—with nations, classes, political parties, governments, industries, interests." We can describe a group of writers, but we cannot explain them as individuals nor can we explain what they did. "Their significant acts, motives, purposes, values, habits, and achievements at the level we are talking about are highly individual," he declared. Being a writer is "a lonely trade," and "the only important thing he does in his whole life, so far as we are concerned, he does alone in a room by himself, quite unobserved." Our skills, he concluded, "are ill-adapted to fathoming the mysteries of [the] human mind in its rare moments of high creativity."[3]

Individual creativity, then, is a "mystery," to use the term Professor Woodward several times prefers. So, too, is collective creativity, including any "Renaissance," wherever and whenever found. We must be skeptical, he warned, of any historian who offers us "his reasons why" any such phenomenon occurred because they are "reasons in a field of endeavor where the nonrational so often holds sway."[4]

Professor Woodward found earlier attempts to explain the Southern Renaissance ill-informed or simply mistaken. Sociologists, "with their special regard for numbers," had tried quantification. Howard Odum, for example, cast a wide net to count five thousand books written by southerners in the first half of the twentieth century. Half were "literature in the traditional sense." Of these, one thousand were fiction, five hundred biography, four hundred poetry, and 125 drama. Striving for some way to measure quality, Odum counted a southerner among Pulitzer Prize winners in more than half of the years since 1917 and found that southerners wrote ten of the eleven best-selling books in the period. Woodward gave more credit for sensitivity to quality to the writer Wilbur Cash than to the sociologists but demolished in detail Cash's idea that Renaissance writers were defending the South against Yankee ridicule.[5]

Having consigned the sociologists to the ash heap and put the flame to Wilbur Cash, Professor Woodward found some value in the thoughts of Vanderbilt Agrarian Allen Tate, writer Robert Penn Warren, and literary scholar Cleanth Brooks. "With the war of 1914–1918," Allen Tate had said, "the South re-entered the world—but gave a backward glance as it stepped over the border: that backward glance gave us the Southern renaissance, a literature of the past in the present." It was "quite temporary," but it "made possible the curious burst of intelligence that we get at a crossing of the ways." For Robert Penn Warren the Renaissance came after 1918 because "the modern industrial world . . . hit the South" and produced "a cultural shock, to a more or less closed and static society." High creativity, Warren thought, came "from this sort of shock, imbalance, need to 'relive,' redefine life." Woodward particularly liked Tate's "backward glance" theory. Even so, he said, it described "necessary conditions," which were "not historical explanations." Cultures, including southern culture, had crossed great divides before without producing a renaissance.[6]

Professor Woodward concluded that "perhaps the historian had best concentrate on necessary conditions and leave causation and explanation to nonhistorians, who are less hobbled by logic." Nevertheless, in an effort to identify which conditions were necessary, he turned to Cleanth Brooks, his friend and colleague at Yale. Brooks had come up with a list of, as he said, "the elements in the life of the South which have an important bearing on its literature." He found six and pointedly numbered each: for example, number 3 indicated "the pervading sense of community"; number 4 pointed to "the sense of religious wholeness." Professors of history, perhaps, hardly needed such enlightenment from a professor of English—even one with a chair at Yale. Woodward quickly improved Brooks's offering out of existence by having him admit that his six scattered shots were "only a few of the many that might have been named" and by having him be "the first to concede" that even his six "had been there a long time—waiting for a Renaissance to happen."[7]

Woodward concluded that critics and literary historians can give us important pointers toward necessary conditions. But there is no end to their number. And even if we did get "a complete and accurate compilation of them, what then?" he asked. Seemingly with the slight shrug that he sometimes used to punctuate his language, he answered: "I am afraid our task of finding the cause of it all would still be a failure."[8]

Without undue immodesty, I think we scholars, including historians, can do a fair job of explaining why there was a tidal wave of creativity in southern culture in the twentieth century. We can explain that phenomenon as well as we have explained why there was an American Revolution in the 1770s or a Civil War in the 1860s. Moreover, I believe we can offer plausible and useful explanations for why a specific artist produced a specific piece of art. Indeed, since—and even before—Professor Woodward published his article in 1975, we have had excellent studies in this area, including books by Richard King, Daniel Singal, Thadious Davis, and Fred Hobson.[9]

If historians have been "hobbled" in the past, it is because we hobbled ourselves, fenced off certain areas and denied ourselves permission even to contemplate its terrain much less trod that ground. "That's not history," a professor, stiff with outrage, might have declared decades ago to a student who proposed some study of William Faulkner's work. Scholars of the same age and mind resisted the idea that there was a history of African Americans more interesting than that of a potato or that there was a history of black-white relations in America worthy of more than cursory attention. Black people were always subordinated to whites and always would be. "First there was slavery," they said flatly, "and then there was segregation."

Vann Woodward was the first white historian who saw clearly that things had not always been the same, that indeed race relations in America had evolved over time in a highly complex fashion. Moreover, in the flux, we whites had too often made the wrong choices. He offered these thoughts in his book *The Strange Career of Jim Crow*, which appeared in 1955.[10] For the great majority of white scholars, it was a revelation, and Martin Luther King Jr. declared it the historical Bible of the Civil Rights movement.

It was as if that book, along with the Civil Rights movement itself, blasted to smithereens a dam and allowed pent-up scholarly concerns to pour out and flood the lands below. Those interests were by no means confined to race relations. Male historians began to understand that women have had a history too. And now we are beginning to realize that there is a history of gender relations and a history of sexual relations—and even homosexual relations—worthy of study.

Perhaps Vann Woodward's greatest gift to humanity was his blasting that dam, opening the field of black-white relations as a legitimate field of study, and thereby making other fields of endeavor accessible to scholars. Paradoxically, race in the long run rules nothing in America. Yet race touches everything—economics, politics, gender, sex, art, literature.

Vann loved irony and paradox as he loved life, because he sensed strongly, I think, the possibility of chaos beneath all things and these were tools to help cope with that possibility. The huge irony in his own life is that his breakout in race relations opened the way for outbreaks in gender and sex relations, consequences that he had neither contemplated nor intended.

Nevertheless, these consequences were fated by the deep history of the South. The mainline southern mind long knew that if the blacks broke out, the women would break out too, and if the blacks and the women broke out, the rednecks would rise and all hell would break loose.

It may be that the greatest revolutions in the study of history come not with new methods such as quantification and the use of the computer, nor with new perspectives such as those provided by Marx and Freud, but rather with the recognition of new subject matter such as race, gender, sex, the Southern Renaissance, and—to emphasize the point—the Renaissance that began in Italy in the fourteenth century. It is our more recent willingness as scholars to contemplate matters of race, gender, and sex that allows us to understand more fully why southern artists and writers in the twentieth century— black and white, male and female—did what they did.

The first generation of the renaissance was born to a Victorian order, and they came to maturity, just as Allen Tate said, in and after World War I, when "modernity" hit the South with a blast. "There isn't much vital imagination," Robert Penn Warren added, "that doesn't come from this sort of shock, imbalance, need to 're-live,' redefine life."[11] That is precisely what, for example, William Faulkner, Margaret Mitchell, and Tennessee Williams were doing. And it is what Elvis Presley represented in the next generation.

The Victorian order was affected by modernity globally, but in the South race made everything different. Victorian society prescribed very clear gender roles for men and women, whether these roles were honored or not. But in the South, especially in the Deep South, the Black Belt South, race vastly exaggerated the Victorian roles. Just as whites had to be whiter than white and blacks blacker than black, so too did men have to be excessively masculine and women exceedingly feminine. Children born to the New South had to find their way to adulthood in a culture in flux, one in which Victorian definitions of true manhood and true womanhood were hotly contested.

We know that William Faulkner, Margaret Mitchell, Tennessee Williams, and Elvis Presley each struggled intensively to realize himself or herself as a sexual creature, to achieve a satisfying presence across the sex line. Each failed in greater or lesser degree. The power of their art is, in a major way, a manifestation of the magnitude of their struggle.

We do not have time to explore the whole life of even one of these artists. But perhaps we can do something useful with elements from the life of Margaret Mitchell, a Georgian who was born in 1900, the very first year of the twentieth century, and lived virtually her whole life in Atlanta, Georgia's most modern city.

We now know undeniably that Margaret as a child of five, almost six, was forced to confront the threat of—as her culture would label it—the "black beast rapist." She was in the very midst of the Atlanta riot in 1906, the most murderous of the many violent eruptions caused by the rapist rhetoric during the turn-of-the-century decades. We know this from three letters written by her father, Eugene, to her mother, May Belle, who was visiting in New York during and after the riot. [12]

In 1906 the Mitchells lived in an elegant two-story Victorian house on Jackson Hill, east of downtown Atlanta. In the bottom between the city and the hill was a community of African American homes, churches, and businesses that the whites called Darktown. Martin Luther King Jr.'s remains now rest in that shallow valley.

All summer the rapist rhetoric had run, and in the late afternoon of Saturday, September 22, 1906, the volcano erupted. Newspapers came out with extra editions announcing one rape after another. Irate crowds gathering on the street corners to discuss the "outrages" began to move to attack passing African Americans.

Margaret's father was a descendant of generations of affluent Georgians, and a lawyer whose specialty was real estate law. Eugene had not fared well in his own real estate ventures during the great depression of the 1890s. Seemingly he was unnerved by his reverses and was overshadowed by his wife, whose fiery red hair was matched by her fiery suffragist rhetoric.

Eugene had worked downtown on Saturday. He had observed then, as he wrote to May Belle on Sunday, "the increasing feeling of the past few days" and noticed unusually large crowds as he came home, but thought little of it. He had gone to bed early but about midnight awoke to the sound of pistol shots in the distance every few minutes and the ringing of the fire bell. Still not alarmed, he went back to sleep.

Sunday morning he was surprised by the news "that 16 negroes had been killed and a multitude had been injured." The mob, he learned, "numbered 10,000 and killed or tried to kill every Negro they saw." Violence touched the Mitchell household itself. Eugene reported that "the cook Estelle came in late and said that her brother had been all cut up."

On Tuesday, Eugene wrote to May Belle again. He thought another outbreak was likely, but assured her that the family was safe. If things got tenser, he would have her mother take the children down to the countryside, near Jonesboro, where she still had relatives.

On the following Saturday Eugene wrote to May Belle again. "Now that the reign of terror has passed," he said, "I can confess that the whole thing has been far worse than the newspapers and dispatches to Northern papers have made it out." The physical violence was awful enough, but the psychological effect was devastating—"the awful terror," as he worded it, "that seized the whole town."

"A thousand rumors were rife," he said, "that Negro mobs had been poised to burn the town, cut the water pipes &c. Sunday night the rumors came thick and fast that Jackson Hill would be burned that night and Slaton and Carroll went down the street warning every man to get his gun and be ready at a moments warning." Slaton was John Slaton, a Jackson Hill neighbor. Interestingly, he would become the governor who in 1915 commuted Leo Frank's death sentence for the murder of "little Mary Phagan" to life in prison and thus triggered Frank's lynching.

Eugene was not prepared for violence. "I had no gun," he wrote, "and could only get the axe and waterkey [a T-shaped metal tool that might be used as a weapon] when Margaret suggested that Mr. Daley's sword would be a good thing." Eugene got the sword and stood—or more probably sat—guard. Just after dark the electric lights went out. Eugene concluded that "the Negroes had cut the wire in darktown." Nearly all the men in the neighborhood sat up. The children were sent to bed, and Eugene's vigil lasted until about 2 A.M. when he too went to bed. "Throughout the night," he said, "pistols and guns would be frequently fired off down in the dip & over about Randolph St."

One can imagine little Margaret, almost six, upstairs in her room and hiding under her bed, as she later said, hearing those pistol shots. She had armed her father as best she could, but she might well doubt his capacity to defend her against a raging—and raping—mob. She might imagine them swarming up the hill from Darktown, creeping into the yard, entering the house and approaching the stairs that led to her bedroom.

When I first read those letters, I thought of the scene in *Gone with the Wind* in which Scarlett confronted the Yankee bummer. On the morning of September 15, 1864, Scarlett was in her upstairs bedroom when she first heard, then saw, the invader enter the yard stealthily. Coolly, she loaded the pistol that her dead husband, Charles Hamilton, had not fired at the enemy during his brief service in the Confederate Army. Charles had been regarded by Scarlett and others generally as a "sissy." Hiding the pistol in her skirts, she began to descend the stairs.

"Who's there?" cried the bummer emerging from the dining room into the hall pistol in hand. "Halt or I'll shoot."

Scarlett froze and the bummer approached.

"So there is somebody ter home," he said, rapidly grasping the magnitude of his advantage and holstering his gun.

"All alone, little lady?" he asked.

"Like lightning," Margaret Mitchell wrote, "she shoved her weapon over the banister and into the startled bearded face. Before he could even fumble at his belt, she pulled the trigger." Scarlett blew a hole in his face where his nose had been—dead center. Then Melanie appeared at the top of the stairs. Exhausted by childbirth and the flight from burning Atlanta, attired in a tattered chemise for a nightgown, she was dragging along the cavalry sword, the saber that had belonged to Scarlett's dead soldier husband who was also Melanie's brother. It was a heavy weapon, one she could barely drag much less lift for effective defense. If Scarlett had not had the pistol, had she not had the strength and courage to use it, both she and Melanie were liable to have suffered, as rapist rhetoric worded it, "a fate worse than death."[13]

An appropriation of fiction for history might imagine Margaret taking the protective role her father should have more persuasively filled during the Atlanta riot. Margaret-as-Scarlett in fiction used the pistol her father did not even have and defended her purity—her "Melanie" as it were. Margaret Mitchell the child might well have asked: "What are men—fathers and husbands—for if not to defend little girls and women from physical attack?" Margaret Mitchell in *Gone with the Wind* might be saying that women must be prepared to defend themselves. In between she was deeply disturbed about sex in her own life.

As a teenage writer, Margaret was virtually obsessed with the rape of young women. As a young woman, she was a self-confessed tease and said that in her own encounters with young men questions of seduction were quickly tabled, and rape was more to the point. She resisted marriage strenuously when all of her friends were marrying. Then, suddenly and to everyone's surprise, she married Berrien "Red" Upshaw, a highly sexed and violent young man half a year younger than she.

Red soon assaulted his bride physically. Margaret's brother and father, both lawyers, eventually had the marriage annulled. Next Margaret married John Marsh, a man who seemed to have been born seventy years old, one whom any girl would love to have as a father. They had no children. She published her book under her maiden name, dedicated it to her husband, but offered only his initials and did not indicate their relationship.[14]

Is the Southern Renaissance over? Was it a phenomenon of only the twentieth century? I think not. More vitally, perhaps, it has been exported to the nonsouthern parts of the nation, along with the outmigration of African Americans, and has entered a new phase. Tensions about race, gender, and sex that created such devastating physical and psychological violence in the South—the homeplace of almost 90 percent of African Americans in 1910—now run riot across the nation with, to say the least, dramatic and shocking results. Witness the responses to the O. J. Simpson–Nicole Brown tragedy in Brentwood, California. The tensions of the Southern Renaissance are still with us, and they are feeding a Northern Renaissance. Already they have produced brilliant work by artists who are not white, not male, and not southern. I think that stream will continue to run riot throughout my lifetime.

NOTES

1. C. Vann Woodward, "Why the Southern Renaissance?" *Virginia Quarterly Review* 51, no. 2 (spring 1975): 222–39.

2. C. Vann Woodward, *Reunion and Reaction: The Compromise of 1877 and the End of Reconstruction* (Boston: Little, Brown, 1951); C. Vann Woodward, *Origins of the New South, 1877–1913,* vol. 7 of *The History of the South,* ed. Merton Coulter and Wendell Holmes Stephenson (Baton Rouge: Louisiana State University Press, 1951).

3. "Why the Southern Renaissance?" 225–26.

4. Ibid., 226–27.

5. Ibid., 223–24, 227–35.

6. Ibid., 235–38.

7. Ibid., 238.

8. Ibid., 238–39.

9. See Richard H. King, *A Southern Renaissance: The Cultural Awakening of the American South, 1930–1955* (New York: Oxford University Press, 1980); Daniel Joseph Singal, *William Faulkner: The Making of a Modernist* (Chapel Hill: University of North Carolina Press, 1997); Thadious M. Davis, *Faulkner's "Negro": Art and the Southern Context* (Baton Rouge: Louisiana State University Press, 1983); Fred Hobson, *Serpent in Eden: H. L. Mencken and the South* (Chapel Hill: University of North Carolina Press, 1974).

10. C. Vann Woodward, *The Strange Career of Jim Crow* (New York: Oxford University Press, 1955). For a highly sophisticated and perceptive presentation of Woodward's life and work, see John Herbert Roper, *C. Vann Woodward, Southerner* (Athens: University of Georgia Press, 1987).

11. "Why the Southern Renaissance?" 235–36.

12. Eugene Mitchell to May Belle Mitchell, 23, 25, 29 September 1906, Margaret Mitchell Marsh Papers, University of Georgia Libraries, Athens. For a more ample treatment of Mitchell, see Joel Williamson, "How Black Was Rhett Butler?" in *The Evolution of Southern Culture*, ed. Newman V. Bartley (Athens: University of Georgia Press, 1988).

13. Margaret Mitchell, *Gone with the Wind* (New York: Macmillan, 1936), 436–40.

14. For a highly creative, penetrating, and deeply researched treatment of Margaret Mitchell's life, see Darden Asbury Pyron, *Southern Daughter: The Life of Margaret Mitchell* (New York: Oxford University Press, 1991). For a close and careful treatment of her relationship with John Marsh, see Marianne Walker, *Margaret Mitchell and John Marsh: The Love Story behind "Gone with the Wind"* (Atlanta: Peachtree Publishers, 1993).

The South as Universe

LINDA WAGNER-MARTIN

Stepping off the cynical and sometimes world-weary planet of the twentieth century—a span of time that seemed to offer all kinds of promise to humankind—I brace my readerly self for what the already-anxious, already-prolific twenty-first century will bring. Armed with the major novels of the turn into the twenty-first century—by such long-established writers as Ralph Ellison, Alice Walker, Harriette Simpson Arnow, Doris Betts, and Tom Wolfe, and such newer talents as Robert Morgan, Charles Frazier, Kaye Gibbons, Barbara Kingsolver, Richard Ford, and Josephine Humphreys—I find myself facing some of the same issues the venerable C. Hugh Holman spoke about in *The Immoderate Past: The Southern Writer and History* (1976).[1]

25

What Professor Holman took on then was a tripartite schema: (1) history, (2) considerations of time, and (3) the omnipresent conundrum of geographic space. For to imagine southern literature is, almost automatically, to invoke history. To define the "southern" mandates drawing the boundary, deepening the already-acknowledged divide, Holman quotes from Allen Tate's proud commentary: "It is scarcely chauvinism . . . to point out that, with the exception of Fitzgerald and Hemingway, the region north of the Potomac and Ohio Rivers has become the step-sister of American fiction."[2] The South, when Tate made his comment in 1959, was fast becoming one of the literary centers of the United States. Despite H. L. Mencken's earlier skepticism, readers the world over understood where great modern letters could be found. It was just before the beginning of that decade, in 1949, that William Faulkner had been awarded the Nobel Prize for Literature.

History as a composite of the past, flooding on and ever toward the present, was one of Faulkner's pervasive themes. With the French and the Russian novelists, with the greatest writers of the West, Faulkner—like Thomas Wolfe, the contemporary southern writer for whom he expressed his highest admiration—aimed to coalesce the meaning of both *pastness* and *history* into a tangible experience, labeled *the present*. Neither great writer (Wolfe or Faulkner) ever explored history for the sake of the exploration; each wanted to capture and present some distillation of that exploration. Holman also quotes Wolfe, that eloquent voice for the deepest concerns of southern letters, when he meditates about time. For Wolfe, writing in 1936, the issue is not to *define* history but rather to move beyond it. Given that there is a present time and a past time, there is also—for Wolfe, the greatest aim—"time immutable, the time of rivers, mountains, oceans, and the earth; a kind of eternal and unchanging universe of time against which would be projected the transience of man's life, the bitter briefness of his day."[3]

As the event of Thomas Wolfe's centenary reminds us, just as his life was brief, so is his reputation—unjustly—proving to be. It *is* a "bitter briefness," and one call to responsible critics who work in southern letters is to put Wolfe back into the paradigm of the great men and women of letters who represented, and represent, southernness. But the fact that Wolfe may have today slipped a little out of that paradigm suggests other ways of looking at the prominence of writers customarily defined as regionalists.

For how do we, today, define a southern writer? Professor Holman used Wolfe as an illustration of the writer's *agon*: "the conflict of time and space."[4] In the hundreds of commentaries already available on "southern literature," the seemingly primary point is definition: who *is* the southern writer? Born in the South—and which states comprise that region? Ones from the nineteenth-century secession, the states defeated in the tragic conflict; or the broader and more economically determined band of states that extend to the equally mythic—but newer—Southwest? So Texas enters, even Oklahoma; but does the line remain to shut out Arizona and Kansas? Is it geography, or is it blood (parents' births? where?), or is it subject matter, or is it spirit? (For example, Holman attributes a great deal of Thomas Wolfe's wanderlust to the fact that his father was born in Pennsylvania.)[5]

John Lowe, in the introduction to *The Future of Southern Letters,* remarks that "there's the question of permanence. Is being southern a category fixed for life? What do you do with the southern writer who leaves the south, both physically and in her fiction?"[6] Can the southern writer shake off Wolfe's warning, go off to make his or her fortune in the East or North, then return to the South and be recognized as a Southerner still? How permanent is the stripe?

In the past fifteen years, the publishing business has made it plain that marketing literature as "southern" has advantages. Eudora Welty and, of course, Carson McCullers, Zora Neale Hurston, Frances Newman, Evelyn Scott, Richard Wright, Ralph Ellison, Lillian Smith, Grace Lumpkin, Olive Tilford Dargan (Fielding Burke), Myra Page,

Robert Penn Warren, Erskine Caldwell, Flannery O'Connor, Margaret Mitchell, Alice Adams, Walker Percy, Sherley Anne Williams, Lee Smith, Cormac McCarthy, Clyde Edgerton, Jill McCorkle, Ellen Gilchrist, John Barth, William Styron, Reynolds Price, Elizabeth Spencer, Allan Gurganus, Ellen Douglas, Wendell Berry, Madison Smartt Bell, Anne Tyler, Nikki Giovanni, Jayne Ann Phillips, Minnie Bruce Pratt, Tim McLaurin, Pat Conroy, Rick Bragg, Randall Kenan, Barry Hannah, Bobbie Ann Mason, Gayle Jones, Dorothy Allison, Beth Henley, Gail Godwin, and on and on—the group of now-defined "southern writers"—has a number of advantages: if readers like a Kaye Gibbons novel, or an *Oldest Living Confederate Widow*, they may buy other fiction similarly marketed. The rubric has expanded—and expanded; the North Carolina Writers' Network now boasts of nearly two thousand annual dues-paying members. As a *Wall Street Journal* headline announced, "*Southern Living* Gets Northern Publisher"[7]; northern publishers make money from publishing *Southern Living*. The South—quaint or vigorous, modest or extravagant, traditional or macabre—has itself become big business (big northern business). And the rest of the world, evidently, wants to read those glossy magazine pages to figure out the tone, the cachet, of the land—a land, as Peter Applebome has told us, that is extremely prosperous and greatly varied. His assessment is that "if the eleven states of the Confederacy were a separate country, it would have the world's fourth largest economy."[8]

There is more to the story of the South today, of course, than its economic prosperity, a prosperity that unfortunately does not touch every southerner. Adrienne Rich speaks to the imaginative hold that southern literature has on today's public and points out some of the dangers of its prominence. In her introduction to Mab Segrest's essays, Rich contends that, "like the Caribbean, or the Middle East, the South is exotic to the rest of the world; for its own people, it is ordinary life—painful, rich, contradictory. When we allow a piece of the world to remain exotic in our imaginations, we dehumanize its people and collaborate in our own ignorance."⁹ This nod to the concept that the South is a kind of monolithic, and therefore limited, culture—an attitude that underlay the disdain of civilized readers early in the twentieth century—points to the strange critical boxes in which southern writers were, and are sometimes still, trapped. Even as late as 1988 Alfred Kazin gives us the monolithic view: "Only the south had known defeat and devastation on its own soil. . . . The hallmark of Southern writing was open resistance to the illusion of unlimited progress."¹⁰ Yet as Lee Smith noted in 1999, set against this conventional literary image, "there's another South, an almost secret South. . . ." About her own career in fiction, especially her early career, she added, "Nobody I knew ever even mentioned the Civil War."¹¹ The problem with literary classifications is that they are drawn from norms: when southern writers are unique in the pervasive literary patterns of the day, they don't "fit," and so they are left outside categorization.

I.

Arguably the most interesting southern writer of the nineteenth century was Edgar Allan Poe, a figure as remotely mysterious as his poetry and fiction. Rather than explore the *literal* geography of his South, Poe created a fantasy world, in comparison with which Faulkner's Yoknapatawpha County looks almost mundane. Striking to readers the world over, Poe's fables of the family romance, the patriarchal dynasty, and the realms of homosocial power foreshadow the tough interrogation twentieth-century southern literature brought to depictions of conventional regionalism. (Might the strangest element of Poe's reputation be that in a culture bent on establishing the value of the American identity, culture, and literature, reifying the existence of the proud New World, his fiction was primarily that of lament for the lost, of anxious fear, at abrupt odds with the "selling" of the United States that other nineteenth-century writers—John Greenleaf

Whittier, Ralph Waldo Emerson, Oliver Wendell Holmes—could be said to have undertaken?)

Even in the works of Samuel Clemens, a southerner of the rascally persuasion (perhaps the start of another tradition?) who used his pseudonym as both disguise and marketing tool, the South takes on a gossamer sheen: is that landscape off the shore of the Mississippi River real or fantasy? Does the vision of lush pristine wilderness have its point of origin here, or in the archetypal imagination of decades of male writers, regardless of region? Is Mark Twain's landscape more central to his fictional world than the characters who people that world? Is his vision throughout his oeuvre as misogynistic as it shows itself to be in *What Is Man?* and the other late, more abstract, pieces?

One might, with good reason, position these two streams of emphasis in nineteenth-century southern writing on opposite edges of the geography the southernist is faced with describing today. On one side is a landscape of natural and fruitful lushness, a metaphor indicative of the rich wildness possible south of the Mason-Dixon Line. On the other is a veritable gallery of characters—and caricatures—many of them illustrating the idiosyncrasies that might continue to flourish in provincial environs. For the South remained a culture of villages and small towns, of farms and wildernesses, much longer than did much of the United States. The existence of the colloquial, even the macabre, in such isolation gave rise to a local-color movement that may be with us still. Kazin says, summarily, of Flannery O'Connor's art: "This emphasis on the smallness and freakishness of human nature was intensely Southern."[12] The often exotic characters that figured the southern landscape were the source of a vein of humor that became known as Southwestern humor (what became of Southeastern humor?), a ribald, crude, and simply funny manner of observing and telling what could pleasantly—or wickedly—be gained from life's experience. The folk—both white and black, lower class and upper—made their presence felt through the literature of the South.

One of the most literary uses of the southern landscape, landscape as mythic, if not outright fictional, force itself, is Thomas Pynchon's *Mason & Dixon* (1997). Although the book is a combination double biography and a formally incongruous eighteenth-century novel, we all supply the word "line" in its title. We American readers will not allow either Mason or Dixon to revert to their Britishness. The object of their exploration, the pivotal focus of their attention, is the American South. Pynchon's primary intent in this novel, however, is to ensure that no one finds the South. Here too it exists in imagination rather than reality; here too it is named but not captured. (Pynchon, of course, is in no way that we know of "southern.")

In southern novels that readers have attended to during the most recent decade, novels that have won National Book Awards and Pulitzer Prizes, this same dichotomy exists: a relentless landscape that is itself cause for valorization, a terrain the reader both absorbs and marvels at, set beside, or sometime against, the writer's intricately etched characters.

It has become current, in popular-culture circles as well as in those of southern intellectual history, to discuss the way these elements of landscape and character function in Margaret Mitchell's 1936 novel, *Gone with the Wind.* Notable as her re-creation of landscape is, Mitchell's more enduring product for the contemporary reader is her characters. Adrienne Rich, however, might call Scarlett O'Hara a stereotype—as we might also point out that many of Mitchell's "southern" characters are pretty "northern." Leaving Rhett Butler out of the equation, the Irish immigrants who are the primary family might just as well have turned right when they came through Pennsylvania as left. Critically, however, while the world knows about *Gone with the Wind* (and its infamous sequel), classrooms abjure it; in the annals of literary criticism, Mitchell does not speak for "southern" literature, at least not in the same quality of voice that Allen Tate's *The Fathers* and William Faulkner's *Absalom, Absalom!* do. Yet, ironically, the "southernness" of U.S. literature cannot escape the depictions of the Civil War that Mitchell created; they are with us permanently and are reflected even as they are deepened and refined in a more recent best-seller, Charles Frazier's 1997 *Cold Mountain*. This impressive first novel has the strengths of landscape and character more evenly balanced than *Gone with the Wind*—one might, in fact, say exquisitely balanced.

Frazier's working out of the Inman-Ada love story—one with a surprisingly more positive outcome than that of the romance in *Gone with the Wind*—allows him to incorporate a number of the elements readers think of as integral to the southern novel and its subgenre, the Civil War novel. What he initially chooses to do is write two narratives, one of the soldier caught in the crucible of horrible bloodshed, the other of the naive woman trying to salvage the land. His alternation of stories is more than plot device, however, for the metaphors of one become the foregrounding of the other: with its narratives as intertwined as strands within an epic poem, *Cold Mountain* provides both point and counterpoint for the attentive reader.

The National Book Award winner for 1998, Frazier's novel sold nearly three million copies in its first year; it has since sold more millions of copies. The liminal metaphor for Inman's journey during, and from, war is the epigraph from Han-shan,

> Men ask the way to Cold Mountain.
> Cold Mountain: there's no through trail. [13]

The words echo William Faulkner's biting dialogue from *The Unvanquished* as the admiring and naive son says to his battle-hardened father, "How do you fight in the mountains, father?" and the answer comes, "You can't. You just have to." [14] As *Cold Mountain* opens, Inman is brushing away flies from "the long wound at his neck" and moves to sit in a chair away from the "broken occupants" of the military hospital. Wounded and near death in a battle outside Petersburg, Inman had been through Malvern Hill, Sharpsburg, and Fredericksburg. He is ready to run.

The novel, from that moment on, is really about landscape—hence its title. From the cartography of the Cold Mountain region—southeast of Waynesville and southwest of Asheville, North Carolina—which provides the endpapers to the book, to Frazier's incremental and persistent use of the mountain's name as the narrative winds to its end, the novel insists that the reader recognize the wonders of the naturally beautiful, uncivilized mountain region. "Mornings on the high bald were crisp, with fog lying in the valleys so that the peaks rose from it disconnected like steep blue islands scattered across a pale sea" (14). That is Inman's recollection as he alternates in his thought between the wisdom he has learned from his Cherokee friend, Swimmer, and his hospital companion, Balis, whose learned meditations end only in death. Frazier makes of Inman the natural philosopher, and he does so by setting him adrift from both civilization and the military with only a tattered and coverless copy of William Bartram's eighteenth-century *Travels* as his Bible. Like the Bible, *Travels* can be opened at random and enjoyed for its pithy, remarkable descriptions of terrain.

> Continued yet ascending until I gained the top of an elevated rocky ridge, when appeared before me a gap or opening between other yet more lofty ascents, through which continued as the rough rocky road led me, close by the winding banks of a large rapid brook, which at length turning to the left, pouring down rocky precipices, glided off through dark groves and high forests, conveying streams of fertility and pleasure to the fields below. (10–11)

The book calms the distraught Inman so that he can sleep, and Frazier shows the way Inman's mind moves from the literal words to his mental imagery of his home: "Cold Mountain, all its ridges and coves and watercourses. Pigeon River, Little East Fork, Sorrell Cove, Deep Gap, Fire Scald Ridge. He knew their names and said them to himself like the words of spells and incantations to ward off the things one fears most."

That William Bartram had been accepted by the Cherokee—indeed, had been named "Flower Gatherer . . . in honor of his satchels full with plants and his attention all given to the growth of wild living things" (10)—brings Inman's sources of humanity into a single identity. Make no mistake, Inman kills throughout the book; that he often does so to protect someone weaker than himself does not lessen the horror of his acts. But the way he finds his humanity again and again is through the language of Bartram. For instance, when he is mired in defeat, certain that he will not find his way back, he reads *Travels* and, in Frazier's careful description, reads it

> pleasurably. . . . First he read [a particularly long sentence] until each word rested in his head with a specific weight peculiar to itself, for if he did not, his attention just skittered over phrases so they left no marks. That accomplished, he fixed in his mind the setting, supplying all the missing details of a high open forest: the kinds of trees that would grow there, the birds that would frequent their limbs, the bracken that would grow under them. When he could hold that picture firm and clear, he began constructing the shrub in his mind. (100–101)

Soothed by his re-creation of his land, Inman is then able to think of the Christmas scene four years earlier when he had begun to make his intentions about her known to Ada.

Inman, an Odysseus without companions or fortune, food or water, and certainly without adventure in any romantic sense, makes his months'-long journey back to Cold Mountain in the most inimical of conditions. He risks his life (and kills three Yankees) to save a pig for a young widowed mother; he avenges the deaths of the town nogoods. He kills to create a higher justice. His daily adventures are interwoven with passages from Bartram to remind the reader how tied to nature, how spiritual, is his quest. Inman's return home is not motivated by monetary profit: its purpose is to nourish and sustain his soul.

One of the most touching scenes in *Cold Mountain* is Inman's turning to the Bartram scroll and offering it to Ada when he has found her once more. His own wordlessness makes him desperate: he finds words in the naturalist's records.

Frazier, of course, also reinforces the primacy of the location by giving Inman, the outlier who sees that his only hope of surviving the war is to return to Cold Mountain and—he hopes—to Ada, this meticulous accounting of the travels of the Bartrams; in the same way, he uses the entire story of Ada, a well-traveled reader but a woman ignorant of living, to show how people must find sustenance in their locale. It is in this domestic novel plot that Frazier shows his understanding of class, privilege, and wisdom: his choosing Ruby, the abused daughter of Stobrod Thewes, to become Ada's guide and instructor is a stroke of great dramatic acuity. What is most important about Frazier's choice is that he avoids any sense of the victim when he draws Ruby—though he brings her father and his companions into the book often enough to let us see that Ruby has little reason to care about Stobrod, despite his wonderful music. Ruby insists that she and Ada be equals. Ada, the landowner, understands the wealth of knowledge Ruby has wrung from the land, and tries to learn it for herself. It is no accident that by the end of Ada and Ruby's narrative, Ada finds it difficult to concentrate on a long British novel that she once would have hungered to read. She has learned that land, food, and people in their reality are the prompts for true human response.

I do not find the designation "feminist novel" used in the reviews of *Cold Mountain*, but Frazier's willingness to give Ada's life half his book shows his politics. Where in southern literature have we had a narrative of two women working the soil, hunting for medicinal herbs, and building fences? Only in Ellen Glasgow's *Barren Ground*, when Dorinda Oakley works with her black employee Fluvanna to make her mother's land profitable for the first time. Given, that book was published in 1925. Today we have issues with racial difference: we don't believe that the two women are friends, and we resent the plotline that makes Dorinda the source of agricultural wisdom (she has read about all the new methods; we are once again faced with an intellectualism made possible by class and travel). Frazier here rewrites that story and makes Ada wise enough to recognize the hard-earned wisdom Ruby has acquired from her own desperately poor, landless majority.

What *Cold Mountain* also provides is a new definition of community, or perhaps *communitas*: Ruby and her younger drifter husband and their children living with Ada and her and Inman's child, a family built from women's comradeship and women's natural roles in the all-too-gendered world. Motherhood is not denigrated here, nor is it privileged. Neither Inman nor Ada seems to have had a mother, and Ruby certainly has not. But the knowledge of how to mother—which Frazier illustrates in the last dramatic scenes of the novel in the women's caring for both Inman and Stobrod, and then of Inman's caring for Stobrod—becomes a quality of humankind not limited to either women or men.

Another, quieter, narrative of the Civil War is Kaye Gibbons's sixth novel, *On the Occasion of My Last Afternoon* (1998). In this re-creation of a North Carolina private hospital during the last years of the war, the power of the narrative comes from Gibbons's vivid evocation of the rule of the white patriarch, the poor-boy-turned-rich-landowner Tate, as he murders his slave Jacob, cutting *his* throat rather than that of the pig the man holds. The novel opens, "I did not mean to kill the nigger! Did not mean to kill him!"[15] Tate's manipulative words poison the life of the community—his family members as well as the slaves on the 1842 plantation—and only Clarice, the African American woman who runs the house, can stand up to him. In the eyes of his twelve-year-old daughter, Emma Garnet, Gibbons's protagonist, Tate is a liar; he remains that. Finally, years after watching her mother endure her father's abuse, Emma marries a northern doctor, Quincy Lowell, and flees—with Clarice—her father's home.

The enormity of the murder of Jacob by his master, the quicksand-like cover-up of the deed, and the community's reaction to it mark

Emma forever. By emphasizing this event, Gibbons gives her readers the Civil War in miniature: such a horrific pattern of abuse cries out for retribution even though people are afraid to call for it or to participate in it. Yet, Emma's sedate tone of voice in recollection in her seventieth year, when she is bereft of parents and husband, softens the stridency of Tate's brutality. Never pastel in its descriptions, *On the Occasion of My Last Afternoon* is something of a watercolor wash—a blurring of separate and separable events that comprise slavery, war, and (as Emma recalls) the fear that writes the script of history. Gibbons makes that point in the passage in which Emma meditates about the difference between her ill-bred father and the kindly neighbor, Mr. Carter, whose family is on a par with that of her mother's:

> Mr. Carter did not enter and curse, did not stomp his displeasure upstairs, did not say "nigger," a word that was expected of the coarse, never mentioned by the gentility, who said "Auntie" or "Uncle," "the servants," "Cuffee," or "the Negroes." And certainly never "slave," though our world would have died in a day without them. I learned through time and the War and eighty-five people to the count dying in my lap that we cannot name what we fear we have made of our lives. For "slave," there was "servant." For the War-dead, the newpapers would head the column "Those Passed at Manassas," "Those Passed at Vicksburg." (26)

In Emma's fusion of pre–Civil War memory and post–, Gibbons stresses the way the acknowledgment of racial difference has shaped definitions of humanity: Mr. Carter is human; Emma's father Tate is less than that. No excuses about his earlier poverty are given validity. What matters is his treatment of the African Americans who are, by law, "his" people. It is interesting that Frazier, because his white characters are themselves poor farmers and not slaveholders, does not touch on any of these racial issues in *Cold Mountain*. He instead posits the Native American, the Cherokee personified in the wise Swimmer and other characters, as the cultural "other."

In keeping with Holman's definition of southern fiction as one that treats the past yet brings it into the present, Gibbons' emphasizes the reason Quincy Lowell has been crucial to Emma Garnet's well-being, even to her sanity: he plays the role of historian to her memories. As Emma says, Lowell is her lover and spouse, her coworker and advocate, he "helped me drag the past into the present, and when I could not maneuver amongst the ruins, he held me steady and helped me step along the roughest places" (35). Since 1987, when she came to prominence as a writer, in none of her fiction has Gibbons blinked the rough places. Whether she is telling the story of an abused child, as in *Ellen Foster,* or of misunderstood women, as in *A Virtuous Woman* or *Sights Unseen,* she provides a candid accounting—though never a sensationalized one—of the trials of the spirit that strong people, usually with help, can survive. *On the Occasion of My Last Afternoon* fits the pattern of her earlier novels, even if it is also a Civil War narrative.

Alice Walker's recent collection of stories, *The Way Forward Is with a Broken Heart,* which is built around "To My Young Husband," the central narrative written in that mix of fiction and seeming autobiography that she has made her own effective form, brings the narrative of racial relations in the South up to the mid twentieth century. Walker's protagonist, an African American woman who has come south in answer to Martin Luther King's exhortations, marries a white New Englander, a civil rights lawyer, and they have a child. Walker's protagonist recalls the child's birth and the reaction of the hospital employees: "No one could believe we were there together, married, to have our neither black nor white child. We were a major offense."[16] Moving from the literal if aphoristic description, Walker dwells on the more colorful image of the young husband's gift of flowers,

> And I remember the red roses, dozens of them, behind which your
> beaming face, later in my room, appeared. The black nurses delighted

in the discomfiture of the white ones, who could not, as the black ones could not, fathom such behavior. Most white fathers of black children in the south never even saw the mothers pregnant, not to mention actually saw the child after birth. The white nurses were soon captivated by your charm and good looks, casting you in the role of a contemporary Rhett Butler, but of course bemoaning the fact that you had chosen the wrong Scarlett. We were the nightmare their mothers had feared, the hidden delight generations of their fathers enjoyed. We were what they had been taught was an impossibility, as unlikely as a two-headed calf: a happy interracial couple, married (and they knew this was still illegal in their state), having a child, whom we obviously cherished, together. (34–35)

Beyond the perhaps expected heterosexual romance, Walker in this collection provides memorable characters—Anne Gray's grandmother, for example, in the story "Conscious Birth" or Miss Mary in "The Brotherhood of the Saved"—who each draws from a collective formed of friendships and love relationships. But finally, what she provides in that first story—and in keeping with the dedication of the book, which is "To the American race"—is a composite of the woman protagonist as a "tri-racial self . . . African, Native American, European" (36). As an inveterate collector of arrowheads and Native American jewelry, the Walker persona traces her own lineage:

My sister, who looks more Cherokee than me, and more European, tells me the Cherokee great-grandmother from whom we descend was herself mad. She was part African. What did that mean in a tribe that kept slaves and were as colorist, no doubt, as the white settlers who drove them from their homes? I do feel I have had to wrestle with our great-grandmother's spirit and bring it to peace. Which I believe I have done. So that now when I participate in Indian ceremonies I do not feel strange, or a stranger, but exactly who I am, an African-AmerIndian woman with a Native American in her soul. And that I have brought us home. (36)

The Walker character goes on to point out how empty of Indians Mississippi is now and how far back into history one must go to find people who originally settled it. In doing so, she evokes a culture that fears difference, profits from it, banishes it, and yet cannot remotely erase its presence: the arrowheads remain, suggestive of the stories and of the lives they embody.

Another Holman, the son of the Holman I have been quoting throughout, made his contribution to the study of southern letters by absorbing the southern into a larger notion of the regional. David Holman's book *A Certain Slant of Light* makes the point that there are "writers who are simply from a geographical region of the country" and then there are writers who are "truly" regional in that they "participate in the communal psychology of the region. . . . their works manifest the values of the region."[17] In turn, "those values inform the world of literature." He concludes, "The regional writer is writing not only *about* the region, but with an awareness gained through experience of what the region . . . a nexus of values, beliefs, and customs [really means]" (14). The thread that draws Charles Frazier, Kaye Gibbons, and Alice Walker together is this sense of intimacy with the region they claim as their South. We feel its—and their—authenticity as we read their diverse stories and the various plots and themes that often trace their paths back to nature and its beauties (as well as its rigors), showing the reader the ways human beings find to live within the social constructions that mark the region.

II.

Reading southern fiction while living in the South is a quintessential experience. Racing from errand to errand, from crowded highway to nonexistent parking space, the reader can leave the burgeoning prosperity of this remarkable 1990s Southland to search for the pace and tone of the legendary South. One finds Thomas Wolfe's "time immutable, the time of rivers, mountains, oceans, and the earth" in a number of recent southern fictions, and within that tonal base a group of what readers must recognize as characteristic southern themes. In the 1999 posthumously published *Juneteenth*—Ralph Ellison's novel that uses the Christian myth as a scaffolding for the story of a white boy's betrayal of the African Americans who raised him—John Callahan, Ellison's literary executor and the editor of this segment of Ellison's last long opus, incorporates passages of truly lyric impact:

> High up the trees flurried with birdsong, and one clear note sang above the rest, a lucid, soaring strand of sound. . . . For a moment we stood there looking down the gentle rising-falling of the land, while far away a cowbell tinkled, small across some hidden field beyond the woods. Milkweed ran across the ground. Imagine to remember—was it ever? Still. Thistle purple-blue, flowers blue, wisteria loud against an old rock wall—was this the season or another time? Certainly there were the early violets among the fallen pine needles—ago too, but that was Alabama and lonesome. [18]

Of Ellison, too, I think we can say that he remained of the South, no matter how far north and east he located himself. *Juneteenth* plays on the keen memory of how crucial religion was and is to the region and of how easily the confirmation of earnest belief might be changed to travesty. Taking the racial issue head on, as he had in *Invisible Man*, Ellison here shows the way a white character might make the kindness of African Americans his plaything. But, as with his earlier novel, *Juneteenth* is seldom as simple as this summary suggests.

With some of his parishioners, the Reverend A. Z. (Alonzo) Hickman has come to the visitor's gallery in Washington, D.C., to see and—he hopes—to meet with the racist senator from New England, Adam Sunraider. While this group of African American Baptists watch, Senator Sunraider (whom they know as the white child Bliss Hickman) is shot many times as he finishes his typically racist speech. A strange congruence of lives sets off the reminiscence of Reverend

Hickman, the preacher who has birthed Bliss in Alabama and then reared him throughout the Southwest to become a puppet of the black church. (Bliss's most fetching and affecting role is to be resurrected from a small white casket, complete with lilies, so that his blond beauty can ensnare the hearts of the African American communities Hickman's traveling ministry visits. The child trickster, like the jazzman-turned-preacher Hickman, manages eventually to trick his way into the U.S. Senate.)

While Hickman realizes how fraudulent his own role in shaping the young Bliss has been, he wonders how a child raised in the goodness of African American communities can become the outspoken, enraging racist of present times. (When Hickman had returned to the Alabama that was the scene of Bliss's illegitimate birth, it was to avenge his brother's lynching and his mother's death. Piety never replaced the anger inherent in his becoming responsible for the white infant. In his own heart, Hickman knows that the current of fraud runs in two directions.)

What Ellison's novel presents is two separate stream-of-consciousness recollections of the prominent, and dying, white senator and the black preacher who winds up watching over the senator as he lies dying in the hospital. Seldom dialogic, the currents of history and memory are fragmented, nonsequential, juxtaposed only in random patterns. Ellison intends that there be no straightforward narrative: the reader's assumption is that all life becomes part of memory and that chronology is one of the irrelevancies that study and intellect have imposed on experience. For instance, as his body weakens, the senator finds himself submerged in a kaleidoscope of visions and dreams: Br'er Rabbit and Br'er Bear are set against sensations of flying, of riding on fast trains, of shooting pigeons and the bets that accompany that contest, and, finally, of the fearful long black car— surely the Cadillac the senator has tastelessly introduced in his speech as the "Coon Cage Eight"—that seems to be coming for him. Iconic narratives of the black experience pepper the matrix of fear-induced conveyances—the speed of a whirling life, or death, gives way on occasion to idiomatic language of jokes, bets, and the dozens.

Before the assassination attempt, Ellison presents the learned Senator Sunraider using the rhetorical devices of the Renaissance court and the smoothly honed languages of the intellectual in his ultimately crass commentary about African Americans. After being shot, however, the senator reverts to Hickman's tone and locution: "Lord, LAWD, WHY HAST THOU . . ." (26). It is only when the preacher Hickman, from the gallery, completes the lament—"FORSAKEN, FORSAKEN, FORSAKEN"—that Sunraider lifts his body to see the man who had reared him and is shot once more.

To the African Americans in the gallery, listening to the speech before the assassination attempt, the senator's unintentional mimicry of Preacher Hickman is cruel parody. As Sister Neal says, ". . . . why, Revere', that's *you*! He's still doing you . . . after all these years and yet he can say all those mean things he says . . ." (34). To Bliss himself, the memory stream of his life is fragmented into ice cream as reward for his "burials," lemonade to ice away the summer afternoons, and the recurring scenes of his romance with Miss Teasing Brown, whose father is part Cherokee. Little sense of the senator's life exists except for his shared history with Hickman. Typical of that shared history is this scene from Bliss's childhood of the church plunged into dark during a storm:

> In the noisy confusion and whirling about Hickman had stamped three times upon the pulpit's hollow floor, shouting, "Sing! Sing!," startling them and triggering some of the singers into an outburst of ragged, incoherent sound. Frightened by the storm, he himself had been crying, but as the old church creaked and groaned beneath the lashing of wind and rain and the screaming continued, the foot-pounding rhythm had come again, this time accompanied by Hickman's lining-out of a snatch of a spiritual in hoarse, authoritative recitative. And suddenly the singers were calmed and the screamers

were silenced and a disciplined quietness had spread beneath the howling of the storm. Then through a flash of lightning he had seen the singers straining towards Hickman who, with voice raised in melody, was stomping out the rhythm on the floor. And as the singers followed his lead and were joined by the nervous choiring of the congregation, he had heard the blended voices rise up in firm array against the thunder. Up, up the voices had climbed until, surrendering themselves to the old familiar words, they were giving forth so vigorously that before his astonished eyes the pitch-black interior of the church had seemed to brighten and come aglow with a joyful and unearthly radiance generated by the mighty outpouring of passionate song. (343)

Juneteenth itself becomes such a "mighty outpouring," and we need only remember Hickman's admonition, that we "stay awake and let the story unfold" (275).

The Ellison novel creates a pair with a better-known fiction from 1998, Barbara Kingsolver's *The Poisonwood Bible.* A Kentucky native, Kingsolver has written powerfully of her childhood in the South, and her short story collection *Homeland and Other Stories* provides ample evidence of the effect of the southern small town on her development as a writer. Because her first novel, *The Bean Trees,* was set primarily in Arizona, Kingsolver was initially marketed as a southwestern writer, but even in the title of that book (the child's name for wisteria, which is hardly a desert plant) she had signaled her point of origin. This is the setting for the title short story "Homeland":

We lived in Morning Glory, a coal town hacked with sharp blades out of a forest that threatened always to take it back. The hickories encroached on the town, springing up unbidden in the middle of dog pens and front yards and the cemetery. The creeping vines for which the town was named drew themselves along wire fences and up the sides of houses with the persistence of the displaced. I have heard it said that if a man stood still in Morning Glory, he would be tied down by vines and not found until first frost. Even the earth underneath us sometimes moved to repossess its losses: the long deep shafts that men opened to rob the coal veins would close themselves up again, as quietly as flesh wounds.[19]

In most of Kingsolver's fiction, however, it is character rather than natural description that absorbs the reader. "Homeland" portrays the great-grandmother's last years, as she—a Native American strangely lost in contemporary society—tries to instill knowledge in her beloved granddaughter. When the child gives her a bouquet of morning glories, Great Mam admonishes her:

> "You shouldn't have picked those. . . . Those are not mine to have and not yours to pick. A flower is alive, just as much as you are. A flower is your cousin. Didn't you know that?"
>
> "I said, No ma'am, that I didn't."
>
> "Well, I'm telling you now, so you will know. Sometimes a person has got to take a life, like a chicken's or a hog's when you need it. If you're hungry, then they're happy to give their flesh up to you because they're your relatives. But nobody is so hungry they need to kill a flower. . . ." (11)

These marvelous characterizations appear in everything Kingsolver writes, and even if *The Poisonwood Bible* appears to be a clearly post-colonial treatment of the Congo during the 1960s, it is also the story of a Georgia couple—the overzealous and autocratic minister and his long-suffering wife—and their four daughters. Taken blindly into the threatening African surroundings, the narrators of the massive novel are the Prices' daughters, each presented with different speech patterns and philosophies in a scheme more rational than, but just as effective as, the one Faulkner created to tell the story of Addie in *As I Lay Dying*. In a way, the daughters' voices are telling the story of their mother, Orleanna Price, the bewildered wife who eventually finds courage enough to claim her children and lead them from the Africa that would change and, perhaps, kill them. In her meditations that open each of the seven sections of the novel, Orleanna privileges her shadowy life on Sanderling Island, at home in her isolation—and her flowering gardens—off the coast of Georgia. Orleanna's "homeland" is again the South.

Like Ellison in *Juneteenth*, Kingsolver here interrogates the power of religion, and the uses to which even the well-meaning are tempted to put that power. Less general critiques of religious beliefs than specific characterizations of one person's abuse of the human yearning to experience religion, both novels give the reader a way to reflect on that pervasive need for solace, for the comfort of belief in a higher being. Ultimately, both novels lead the reader to that solace in a human community. Revisionist, in that writing about religion has ceased to be fashionable, these books open areas of controversy to readers who have long lamented the loss of serious fiction that deals with philosophical and religious beliefs.

Kingsolver's recent novel, *Prodigal Summer*, treats religion less obviously, turning instead to three narratives set in the near-wilderness of southern Appalachia. Farmers' lives in Zebulon Valley are hard, but few starve: people supplement their farming income with earnings from other jobs. In the central narrative of the Widener family and its farm, deeded to Cole, the youngest child and only son, Kingsolver describes the persistence, and inventiveness of learning to work the land. When Cole marries Lusa Maluf Landowski, a postdoctoral scientist whose parents are a Polish Jew and a Palestinian, the Widener world is drastically changed. Lusa, becoming as committed to saving the farm as the family has been, explains to the youngest sister, Jewel, why there will be no lumber harvest: because she loves "the trees, the moths. The foxes, all the wild things that live up there. It's Cole's childhood up there too. Along with yours and your sisters'." [20]

The other two narratives concern the forest and its inhabitants more directly: Garnett Walker's story is of his preserving the seed of the chestnut tree, a metaphoric evocation of his family's land, and learning to live with his grandchildren and his neighbor; Deanna's story is of her return to a human life after isolating herself in the forest preserve, a voluntary exile, to maintain its animals and to avoid the troubles of her lost marriage. *Prodigal Summer* is filled with detailed descriptions of moths, coyotes, turtles, snakes, birds, and the vegetation that surrounds them. As fascinating as Kingsolver's intricate layering of description is, the novel becomes yet a larger statement of the way human beings, too, find community—often through understanding the reverence in which others hold the natural world. In this plotline, Lusa's relationship with Jewel's daughter Crys (a girl often mistaken for a boy) and her younger brother, Lowell, cements the more suggestive commentary of the other two stories.

A 1930s novel published for the first time in 1999, Harriett Simpson Arnow's *Between the Flowers* is another text that questions the place of religion, and of the natural world, in people's humble lives. The impoverished Marsh defines his American dream as land ownership; he first wins and then loses his beloved Delph as he allows their life together to become one of foolishly dangerous acquisitions. Delph, one of Arnow's winningly independent women, comes from a prosperous family: she does not marry for position, but rather for love. The role of religion is subtle here but, as in Arnow's other important books, crucial. For all her high spiritedness, Delph bears the will of the community within her, and even though her marriage is disappointing, she feels guilt at her withdrawal: "It had seemed sinful and flying in the face of God not to have children when she lived with Marsh as his wife."[21]

As Delph watches the man she married become the product of too many hard days in uncompromising fields, facing the terrible backbreaking hardness of life on a poor farm, "she thought of Marsh as he had been, and as he was now—no better than a plant of wilting corn. She could have cried for him, but he didn't want her tears. He didn't want her; he wanted the land . . ." (200). And Marsh in turn realizes that his wife has—at least spiritually—left him, "a part of her leaping away, flying over his head while her body remained in his arms . . .

the rest of her was like an unseen, unfelt wind that moved clouds a man could hardly see" (354). Never a simple romance, Arnow's novel is the record of the embodiment of the way community, with its undergirding of the spiritual, creates—and enforces—a homogeneity that may sacrifice its brightest and its best. What Kingsolver's *Prodigal Summer* adds to Arnow's tapestry of women's lives rarely lived separate from man's is a range of women characters who have found the will and the resources to define useful lives as satisfying ones.

III.

Had I the time or space to move back to the early 1990s, I would rehearse the impact of the novels of several other contemporary southern women writers, such as Lee Smith and Jill McCorkle. Like the somewhat earlier novels of Ellen Gilchrist, Ellen Douglas, and Doris Betts, the work of these writers captures the immediacy of modern life—and its frequently unpleasant plots as marriages crumble, child care needs mount, and finances vanish. The choices women characters must make in *Tending to Virginia, Ferris Beach, Family Linen, Oral History,* and *Fair and Tender Ladies* become the universalizing themes that make these southern narratives stories of today's Everywoman. What Patricia Yaeger defines in her recent *Dirt and Desire* as fiction "filled with a litany of objects that, in their exoticism, localism, and eccentricity, seem designed to provide . . . a southern 'reality' effect" is more of a norm than it is a regional trait.[22]

In 1985 Mab Segrest called for just those effects, predicting that "the future of Southern literature depends on the female imagination, on female creative energy that is already spinning a new Southern writing."[23] To look back these past fifteen years is to see shelves of women's fiction about family, society, love relationships, and hate, histories claimed from a perspective more personal than cultural, the whole easily, and sometimes saucily, voiced in the locutions of both storytelling and everyday dialogue. It is no small accomplishment, and it depends for its point of origin on the great variety and wealth of fiction by Eudora Welty, Elizabeth Spencer, Carson McCullers, and Flannery O'Connor.

Michael Kreyling, in his 1998 *Inventing Southern Literature,* identifies what he terms "three of the most pressing issues arising in southern literary study," and one of those issues is "construing the white southern woman's tradition(s) as affirming the orthodox idea of southernness."[24] Rather than continuously omitting the southern woman writer from the canon, or finding that she belongs within some separate lineage, Kreyling rightly wants incorporation. But as Susan V. Donaldson and Anne Goodwyn Jones have pointed out in their introduction to *Haunted Bodies: Gender and Southern Texts,* considerations of gender, particularly in assessments of southern literature, are often oversimplified:

> The assumption of a special clarity and permanence about *southern* gender evident in time-honored stories of white cavaliers and belles, of black Jezebels and rapacious Nat Turners, might well owe its origin and persistence, then, to general unease with the sometimes intense and always unending negotiations defining gender within the region. Such stories may have appeared all the more reassuring in a region where manhood and womanhood seemed so difficult to control. By the same token, such stories may have falsely reassured nonsoutherners that a simpler world existed elsewhere.[25]

One cannot just put women writers into the mix and have the categories—whether they be romance, war, religious and philosophical treatise, travel, racial commentary, or whatever trope—remain static. As Patricia Yaeger somewhat harshly, and at significant length, determines, much of the commentary that exists about writing by southern women either glosses over the real characteristics of that work or buries those qualities.[26]

The phenomenon of Robert Morgan's *Gap Creek,* a novel about a strong woman character, a book raised to bestsellerdom by being selected for the Oprah Book Club (as were Kaye Gibbons's first novels, in tandem, and Barbara Kingsolver's *The Poisonwood Bible*), illustrates Yaeger's criticism of the way novels about women (as well as novels written by women) are themselves stereotyped. In predicting that Morgan's protagonist, Julie Harmon, will survive the incredibly difficult first year of her marriage—that she will triumph over nature, circumstances, and a thoughtless young husband, not to mention literal flood and fire—the reader accepts the conventions of the domestic novel. Few books imperil their women protagonists so severely as Morgan does his Julie, and one might comment that the novel borders on the sensational, using the hardship of the Appalachian highlands to create a text that is nearer melodrama than tragedy.

With an ironic twist of readers' acceptance, Morgan's Julie may be convincing at least partly because she is the creation of a male writer. Free of the suspicion about novels by women that have so-called political themes, *Gap Creek* may well become the choice for people who want to read realistic fiction about the poor and hardworking—again, in part because it is a narrative about life on the marginal farms of the South, and much of the readers' attention falls on the detailed descriptions of rending lard, for instance, or killing chickens. Morgan repeats the concept of the exotic, however, in his insistence that Julie works so hard and is able to use her strength so efficiently because she is manlike.

Kreyling's other two considerations are also worth our attention. He first of all questions the role of the male African American writer and asks whether or not such a writer as Richard Wright or the Ellison of *Invisible Man* can legitimately speak for the South or for only a terribly marginalized view of the region. Like Fred Hobson, Kreyling suggests that what twentieth-century literary critics see as the marginalized view may, in fact, be the primary view.[27] Perhaps adding to the mix Ellison's *Juneteenth*, and considering that novel along with works by more contemporary male African American southern writers, would provide contextualization for the question.

Kreyling's last issue is his challenging critics of southern literature to determine the role of William Faulkner's fiction as they consider how southern literature today is both defined and judged.[28]

There is, of course, no other southern writer whose art has changed the path of all literature in English—and beyond. Faulkner *is* the twentieth-century novelist to be reckoned with: he must be studied; his greatness must be acknowledged; his influence must be allowed. Of all the writers whose work has a great deal in common with his, the most visible today are the nonsoutherner Toni Morrison and the southerner who risks being lost in that shifting set of boundaries between the South and the Southwest, Cormac McCarthy. In his pervasive and skillful creation of stunningly bleak landscapes—and the tattered human lives that live within them—McCarthy is unique.

He is also frightening. If Faulkner's vision was ever so nihilistic, perhaps the convolutions of his narrative method kept readers from seeing the emptiness at the end of the story. Spread among parallel plots and juxtaposed characters, Faulkner's most somber messages yet seemed enlivened by his extraordinary gifts of language. For McCarthy, however, who tends to pour his immense verbal power into one story line, the impact of an unwise choice is relentless. As John Cawelti has recently summarized McCarthy's characters, they are "driven by a restlessness and a desperation of spirit that urged them on to glorious accomplishment or catastrophic destruction."[29] It is the ashes of that destruction that so often mark a McCarthy work.

Cormac McCarthy is the southern writer students most often ask about—the mantle of Faulkner rides easily on his shoulders, most visibly in the earlier work. The 1968 *Outer Dark*, for example, is built from the catatonically elliptical segments of the Holmes siblings' narrative concerning Culla and Rinthy and their ill-gotten child. In this story of such deep poverty, illiteracy, and moral and religious ignorance, McCarthy might be compared to the Faulkner of *As I Lay Dying,* but whereas Faulkner viewed his characters as feebly quaint, McCarthy makes us flinch at the bedrock of meanness that governs his so-called civilization. The depravity in this and in most of his novels accrues in characters other than the Holmeses, however; for in McCarthy's world the prize goes to the utterly *in*humane. The monsters that appear in nearly every scene did not exist in most of Faulkner's Yoknapatawpha County.

By the time of *Blood Meridian or the Evening Redness in the West* (1985), this full-blown presence and power of the depraved is what remains of the mock-historical novel set in the 1849–1850 Southwest United States and Mexico. As the kid, who is a fourteen-year-old Tennessean at the book's opening, matures into a wasted, godless human, the reader pulls back from his or her initial identification with the poor, lost child. But more of the novel concerns the demented John Glanton and the erudite, hairless giant, Judge Holden, and their business of selling Indian scalps. Whenever McCarthy changes the narrative trope, it is for the effect of devastation, never comedy. As Cawelti sees McCarthy's development, moving in his fiction "from the heart of the South to the edges of the West," his progression is to show a great deal about the South. In the critic's summation, "the South was founded by a horde of restless seekers who left their home places behind them in pursuit of a plethora of dreams."[30] That the tenor of those dreams is more Conradian than Horatio Alger–like is Cormac McCarthy's contribution to southern and to American letters.

IV.

It is in many ways reassuring that much southern fiction of the 1990s does, in fact, attempt to capture some essential American dream. Whether it be the search for home as Delia Byrd and her daughters return to Cayro, Georgia, in Dorothy Allison's 1998 *Cavedweller*, or Charlie Croker's fight to maintain his extravagant Atlanta-based lifestyle in Tom Wolfe's *A Man in Full* the same year, or the somewhat more moving odyssey Richard Ford's Frank Bascombe (sportswriter turned real estate salesman) takes toward fatherhood in the 1996 Pulitzer Prize–winning *Independence Day,* readers of the range of southern fiction are reminded of what being human means. The terrain may be more frequently urban than rural, but the impulse to partake of a community transcends that geographical distinction. As this sweep through recent fiction has tried to suggest, the craft of writing still pushes toward the idealistic goal stated so beautifully by our first Thomas Wolfe: the creation of "time immutable, the time of rivers, mountains, oceans, and the earth; a kind of eternal and unchanging universe of time against which would be projected the transience of man's life, the bitter briefness of his day"—the South as universe.[31]

NOTES

1. C. Hugh Holman, *The Immoderate Past: The Southern Writer and History* (Athens: University of Georgia Press, 1977).

2. Allen Tate, "A Southern Mode of the Imagination," in *Essays of Four Decades* (Chicago: Swallow, 1968), 578.

3. Thomas Wolfe, *The Story of a Novel* (New York: Scribner's, 1936), 51–52.

4. Holman, *The Immoderate Past,* 98.

5. Ibid.

6. John Lowe, introduction to *The Future of Southern Letters,* edited by Jefferson Humphries and John Lowe (New York: Oxford University Press, 1996), 5.

7. Erin White, "*Southern Living* Gets Northern Publisher," *Wall Street Journal,* 4 August 2000.

8. Peter Applebome, *Dixie Rising: How the South Is Shaping American Values, Politics, and Culture* (New York: Random House, 1996), 9.

9. Adrienne Rich, introduction to *My Mama's Dead Squirrel: Lesbian Essays on Southern Culture,* by Mab Segrest (Ithaca: Firebrand, 1985), 14.

10. Alfred Kazin, *A Writer's America: Landscape in Literature* (New York: Knopf, 1988), 144, 143.

11. Lee Smith, "Far from the Marble Generals," *Women's Review of Books* 16, nos. 10–11 (July 1999): 21.

12. Kazin, *A Writer's America*, 150.

13. Charles Frazier, *Cold Mountain* (New York: Atlantic Monthly Press, 1997), epigraph page. Hereafter cited in text.

14. William Faulkner, *The Unvanquished*, in *William Faulkner: Novels 1936–1940*, ed. Joseph Blotner and Noel Polk (New York: Library of the Americas, 1990), 330.

15. Kaye Gibbons, *On the Occasion of My Last Afternoon* (New York: G. P. Putnam's, 1998), 1. Hereafter cited in text.

16. Alice Walker, *The Way Forward Is with a Broken Heart* (New York: Random House, 2000), 34. Hereafter cited in text.

17. David Marion Holman, *A Certain Slant of Light: Regionalism and the Form of Southern and Midwestern Fiction* (Baton Rouge: Louisiana State University Press, 1995), 13.

18. Ralph Ellison, *Juneteenth*, ed. John F. Callahan (New York: Random House, 1999). Hereafter cited in text.

19. Barbara Kingsolver, "Homeland" in *Homeland and Other Stories* (New York: HarperCollins, 1989), 2. Hereafter cited in text.

20. Barbara Kingsolver, *Prodigal Summer* (New York: HarperCollins, 2000), 123.

21. Harriette Simpson Arnow, *Between the Flowers*, ed. Fred Svoboda (East Lansing: Michigan State University Press, 1999), 355.

22. Patricia Yaeger, *Dirt and Desire: Reconstructing Southern Women's Writing, 1930–1990* (Chicago: University of Chicago Press, 2000), 201.

23. Mab Segrest, *My Mama's Dead Squirrel: Lesbian Essays on Southern Culture* (Ithaca: Firebrand, 1985), 19.

24. Michael Kreyling, *Inventing Southern Literature* (Jackson: University Press of Mississippi, 1998), xiv.

25. Susan V. Donaldson and Anne Goodwyn Jones, introduction to *Haunted Bodies: Gender and Southern Texts* (Charlottesville: University Press of Virginia, 1997), 6–7.

26. Patricia Yaeger, *Dirt and Desire*; see especially chapters 1 and 2.

27. See Fred Hobson, *The Southern Writer in the Postmodern World* (Athens: University of Georgia Press, 1991), 101.

28. Michael Kreyling, *Inventing Southern Literature*, xiv.

29. John G. Cawelti, "Cormac McCarthy, Restless Seekers," in

Southern Writers at Century's End, ed. Jeffrey J. Folks and James A. Perkins (Lexington: University Press of Kentucky, 1997), 164.

30. Ibid., 165.

31. Thomas Wolfe, *The Story of a Novel*, 51–52.

Sashaying through the South

THADIOUS M. DAVIS

I. Excursion

The "South" of my title has porous boundaries, which when combined with a verb of movement, "sashay," speaks directly to a fluidity that may not be immediately apparent. It encompasses a largely unregulated spatial designation and an unruly temporal location out of which meaning has been coerced. Put another way, it is a tense coupling of ideology and psychology simultaneously fast dancing and slow dragging toward an unsustainable and perhaps undesirable equilibrium. A flirtatious, sexual motion or connotation suggested by this description is intentional, because the coming together signals a move toward a reproductive process out of which will emerge one version of twenty-first-century southern literary production.

If this introduction sounds at once vaguely abstract and irreverently playful, that too is intentional, because one of the prominent markers of much twenty-first-century southern writing is that it is humorously self-reflexive in and unself-consciously delighted by the interplay of language and ideas. It is often metafictional, as in the writing about the writing of fiction, no matter what the specified genre may be, and as such, it makes no effort to conceal its motive or its pleasure derived from words, narrative, and language addressing and engaging the production of writing itself.

I think of the title, too, as a prancing, dancing, playful iconography of the familiar defamiliarized. It stems both from the sound of the term sashay and its aural relation to the name Shay, as in Shay Youngblood, and from the sense of the term and its literal dictionary definition:

SASHAY *intransitive v. informal.* 1. To strut or flounce. 2. To perform the chassé in dancing; *n. informal.* An excursion; a sally [variant of Chassé].

CHASSÉ n. A dance movement consisting of one or more quick, gliding steps with the same foot always leading. Intr. v. chasséd, -séing, -sés. To make or perform this movement. [French, from the past participle of *chassér*, to chase, from Old French, *chacier*, to chase.[1]]

The forward glide of the *chassé* effectively foregrounds the movement into the new and the next, and the strutting or flouncing motion of the dance, one carrying a male gender signature and the other a female one, though the two are also unisex, evokes the attitude or posture of the writers whose movement carries us forward.

The title's verbal play also originates in my own cultural and familial history. It echoes my great-grandmother's "*ça va, cher,*" which almost always sounded like "shay," though perhaps with a slightly shorted "a" or "eh" sound. Thus, the term "sashaying" becomes a trope for the mixture of languages, words, meanings, and sounds that for me have always been part of my being in and of a South. In the play of language, I now take my great-grandmother's colloquial Creole, "How are you, dear?" to signify the question implicit in focusing attention on "the South in the twenty-first century."

At a moment in the 1980s when I felt the exterior spaces I identified as South places were too varied and different to collapse into the usable and all too familiar designation, I read C. Hugh Holman's "No More Monoliths, Please: Continuities in the Multi-Souths," his last essay before his death. That essay opened a space that corresponded with my rethinking what "South" meant in a multidimensional fashion very much in keeping with the specific cultural resonances of the New Orleans of my birth and upbringing. While I had never been able to think of a South in strictly homogeneous terms, I had been unable to articulate why the South lacked a totalizing meaning and thus imaginative force for my interpretation of southern culture and southern literature. In specifically calling for a greater recognition of "a profoundly pluralistic world," Holman commended the work of black studies, feminist studies, and critical theory for "casting fresh illumination on southern literary culture."[2] Observing the change brought about by the inclusion of black writers into assessments of southern culture, Holman welcomed "these new and vital forces":

> It is not merely that we are at last looking at slave narratives, giving Frederick Douglass his long overdue place in southern letters, and examining Charles Chesnutt as an artist rather than a curiosity. A number of writers of great importance are entering the canon—such as Ralph Ellison, Richard Wright, Ernest Gaines, and Ishmael Reed. When they enter, they greatly increase the meaning of southern culture, enrich the themes of southern writing, introduce new experiences of their own, and give new perspectives by which to judge the old.[3]

Despite its seeming suggestion that all black writers are men, Holman's call for recognition of variety in southern culture, for a change in attitudes, was not an isolated position in the 1980s, when black studies, women's studies, and emergent theoretical and cultural studies were compiling scholarly records and research to challenge and subvert old paradigms about the South. More recently, the sociologist Larry Griffin's essay "Southern Distinctiveness, Yet Again, or, Why American Still Needs the South" (*Southern Cultures,* fall 2000) has provided a virtual compendium of both the old paradigms of the South and the new conceptual reconfigurations of the "multi-South." Griffin understands that the question now is "Which South?" or "Whose South?" and that all answers are relative and constructed.[4]

II. Sashay

The last two decades of the twentieth century, in fact, witnessed a pronounced seedbed of changes in the literature in, of, and/or about the multi-South, now so "multi" that Robert Olen Butler's writing on the Vietnamese in Louisiana is no more a curiosity than Ernest Gaines's Cajuns and Creoles, or Judith Ortiz Cofer's narratives of growing up Puerto Rican in Georgia.

In the process of these changes, what we know as southern literature has been undergoing major transformations. Slowly and perhaps imperceptibly, the tenets defining and codifying fiction, poetry, and drama under the familiar rubric have been loosening and dissipating, because they often are simply ignored, whether from conscious intentionality or from simple unknowing (ignorance). The breaking down of barriers, symbolically located in the breaking up of the institution of segregation, the Jim Crowism that divided and defined the pre-1960s South, has produced a less walled-off, less isolated region into which people of color from Mexico, Puerto Rico, Latin and South America, from Cuba and the Caribbean Islands, from India, Vietnam, South and Southeastern Asia, and postcolonial Africa could figure and could, in fact, exist in less problematic circumstances than before the felling of the color bars visibly separating blacks and whites and, by extension, virtually sealing the region from entry by other people of color who would in effect be subject to the same restrictive covenants as black people of African descent.

Just as an aside, the same practices of segregation also precluded the identification of Native American people as other than white in the South. When Alice Walker included "Motheroot," a poem by the Tennessee Cherokee writer Awiakta as the epigraph to *In Search of Our Mothers' Gardens* (1983), she slid across the black-white racial binary characterizing the literature associated with the South. Born in 1936 in Knoxville, Tennessee, Marilou Awiakta Bonham grew up in Oak Ridge, Tennessee, where scientists conducted nuclear experiments in splitting the atom. Today, she self-identifies as an Indian, as a woman of color, and as a southerner. In the late 1970s, there was little demand for her book *Abiding Appalachia: Where Mountain and Atom Meet* (1978; 1994), a stunning collection of poems mediating scientific thought about nuclear power and Cherokee myths of reverence for all life. However, when it was reissued in 1994, both its commentary on a specific environmental aspect of southern living and her status as a member of the Eastern Band of the Cherokee Nation, those who refused to be herded West on the Trail of Tears, made it an award-winning work, which has also been the case with her *Selu: Seeking the Corn Mother's Wisdom* (reissued by Quality Paperback Book Club in 1994). Though Awiakta, whose name in Cherokee means "eye of the deer," has now received some recognition as a recent southern writer, her dates of first publication place her within the lost generation of those who were not classified as southern, because all the southern writers were white, and mainly men, and could barely, if at all, make their living in the writing profession.[5]

I might add, too, that there is a marked similarity between Awiakta and Sybil Kein, a Louisiana Creole who writes in Creole, French, and English. Born in 1939, Kein self-identifies as African American, but has insisted also on being Creole and recovering the Creole language in the poetry and prose and songs she produced throughout the 1960s and 1970s. Her book of poetry *Gombo People*, first published in 1981, was reissued in an expanded edition in 1999. Her elegant poems in Creole and English appear in her 1996 collection, *An American South*.

Only in the 1980s and 1990s did Kein begin to receive attention as a southern woman writer of color who complicates conventional notions of race and of language and of region, whose aesthetic and creative traditions, like those of Awiakta, do not adhere to a traditional black-white binary.

The larger American reading public, nonetheless, may still have a desire to have the South fixed and frozen in imagination, aesthetics, and race. And southerners themselves may have a desire for the familiar, the comfortable, the nonthreatening, even when the imagistic power has been dissipated by overexposure. Somehow, the televisual possibilities from the *Beverly Hillbillies* to *The Waltons* still seem to say "the South" and "southern literature." It may be no accident that Mark Childress's *Crazy in Alabama,* in which Lucille leaves the South to star in *The Beverly Hillbillies* in Los Angeles and in which her twelve-year-old nephew, Peejoe, discovers the separate meanings of southern justice, was made into a motion picture. While echoes of Scout in *To Kill a Mockingbird* are not unwelcomed, there is a point at which the lynch mob and the white child's response to racial injustice become redundant. Ernest Gaines, in *A Lesson Before Dying,* like Bebe Moore Campbell in *Your Blues Ain't Like Mine* or Albert French in *Billy,* will take us back to the historical South of brutal lynchings, incarcerations, electrocutions, and racism that speaks to the dehumanization of the perpetrators as well as the victims; yet recalling Scout's learning curve does not seem to be part of the plot, but new or rather previously unnamed violence is. Clearly, too, *Gone with the Wind*— with its scheming belle Scarlett, its dashing scoundrel Rhett, its ever-present Tara, its beaming Mammy and skittish Prissy, its fiery images of Atlanta burning, and the destruction of the Civil War—speaks to the historical South. That South is not far from *Cold Mountain* and Charles Frazier's award-winning representation of the characters who lived large during the crisis of war, though the seemingly new twist is that they are ordinary working-class people, just plain mountain folk outside the plantation and slaveholding culture of that other South.

While there may be a nostalgic yearning for the familiarity of comfortable southern books, those that fit like old slippers or worn gloves or, in particular, like men's baseball gloves, as in the case of Tony Earley's coming-of-age novel *Jim the Boy* (2000), with its decidedly male and back-looking gender signature, there is also a strong movement toward the new, the different, the now that addresses not only the present but the future literature of the South.

The distinction between commercial and popular fiction and quality serious literature has been breaking down. Commercial success is what fuels the writing as much as the publishing and marketing of books. Oprah's Book Club has more power in the publishing world than a savvy editor at a reputable house. And who is to say that reading tastes ought not to be shaped and indulged by Oprah, her staff, and Harpo Productions? Without them, the Georgia resident, playwright, and novelist Pearl Cleage would have seen her novel *What Looks Like Crazy on an Ordinary Day* disappear from print after a small initial run. The marketing of certain representative voices, such as Maya Angelou, Ernest Gaines, Alice Walker, or Yusef Komunyakaa, or even Albert French and Reynolds Price, Lee Smith, Jill McCorkle, Clyde Edgerton, and Kaye Gibbons, happens simultaneously with those of Rebecca Wells and her *Divine Secrets of the Ya-Ya Sisterhood*, Connie May Fowler's *Before Women Had Wings*, and Dorothy Allison's *Bastard out of Carolina*. Humor and pain, women's friendships and betrayals coalesce in the taking to a large public audience some of the secret, private realities of girl- and womanhood within the context of the culture of the South and in the long-buried narratives that deconstruct the pedestal. Gibbons's *Ellen Foster* and Dori Sanders's *Clover*, like Lee Smith's *Saving Grace*, all take on adolescent maturation as female with southern cultures of sexism and oppression, religion and violence, and all give us narratives not fully possible just a few decades ago because there is an interest in thematic representations of certain cultural issues—be they race, gender, religion, or class. Julie Smith's mystery series set in New Orleans, with a detective based in the French Quarter, and James Lee Burke's set in bayou country are as equally on our radar of southern writers as James Wilcox or Nancy Lehmann in their narratives of Louisiana. Pat Conroy's *The Great Santini* and *The Prince of Tides*, like Anne Rice's vampire series, are made into films and signal to others that Hollywood movie options and film adaptations are indeed not only possible but profitable. Though Richard Wright has an expatriate heir in Barbara Chase-Riboud, her writings, from *Echo of Lions* to *The President's Daughter* and *Sally Hemings: A Novel*, are committed to history in a way Wright's are not; Wright could never admit the past into his vision or tolerate the shape of then with his creation of now. The collapsing of a distinction between the literary and the popular, and the resultant commercialization, have had an impact on the literature and images of the South.

In casting an eye here on young writers, I do not mean to leave off the chassé card any of the writers who are busily producing the extraordinary literature we call southern: Eudora Welty, Elizabeth Spencer, Shirley Ann Grau, the brave Ellen Douglas, Beth Henley, Alice Adams, Rita Mae Brown, Fannie Flagg, James Alan McPherson, Ann Allen Shockley, Larry McMurtry, Cormac McCarthy, Ellen Gilchrist, Gail Godwin, Colleen McElroy, Pinkie Gordon Lane, Doris Betts, Mary Hood, Harry Crews, Gerald Barrax, and Lorenzo Thomas all continue to strut and flounce, to dance their dance. Larry Brown, Mary Ward Brown, Lewis Nordan, Pam Durban, Kalamu ya Salaam, Linda Beatrice Brown, James Seay, Sallie Bingham, Robert Gingher, Brenda Marie Osbey, Rosellen Brown, Sterling Plumpp, Elizabeth Brown-Guillory, Joan Williams, and perhaps Anne Tyler as well, if we still consider her southern, are all part of the motion of creation and the shape of the dance. This list is not intended to be exhaustive but merely suggestive though also somewhat representative. Many of the writers in the southern canon, such as Bobbie Ann Mason, Josephine Humphreys, Jayne Anne Phillips, Naomi Shihab Nye, Padgett Powell, Gayl Jones, Jill McCorkle, Lee

Allison Wilson, John Grisham, Gwendolyn Parker, Robert Olen Butler, and Lee Smith, will, of course, be in their writing maturity and imaginative prime in the twenty-first century.

Even writers who have been silent for a decade cannot be counted out. Gayl Jones returned at the end of the 1990s with two impressive forward-looking novels, *The Healing* and *Mosquito*. Her novel *Mosquito* (1999) is, for example, six hundred pages of Sojourner Nadine Jane Johnson's voice challenging and exploding typecasting. She is a truck driver pausing to tell her story in a South Texas bar where her Chicana friend, Delgadina, works. As if a black woman truck driver is not stereotype-bending enough for Jones, she then creates Mosquito, a political worker in a sanctuary movement for Mexican immigrants. Exhibiting amazing verbal dexterity in her expansive language and verbal play, Mosquito in her signifying and specifying also demonstrates the characteristic that Zora Neale Hurston termed "wide-picture" talking. The powerful and humorous oral narrative she unfolds is southern porch-talking taken to another level. As marvelous a gift to our literature as Jones and these exemplary writers are collectively, they are, nonetheless, not the ones I would like to address.

III. Sally

Born at the end of the 1950s in the aftermath of *Brown v. Board of Education* and in the 1960s and 1970s, the younger writers know both a racially mixed world and a racially homogenous one. They came of age when socially transformative movements, the Civil Rights movement, the women's movement, and—the one less frequently mentioned on equal grounds—the computer movement, empowered lives. Writers who have emerged since the era of integration in the South and the writers who will make the literature we may still call southern in the twenty-first century are diverse, sassy, and savvy. Poets such as Natasha Trethewey, Mona Lisa Salloy, T. J. Anderson III, and Kevin Young, novelists such as Donna Tartt, Tina McElroy Ansa, Evelyn Coleman, Shay Youngblood, and Randall Kenan do not constitute an inclusive list; rather, they are not even a small fraction of the youngsters writing and publishing today who have formidable connections to the South. These younger writers have come of age when they have the freedom to define themselves and their work in more than regional or racial terms. They may define their subject positions as multiply intersectional with gender and sexuality, religion and class, as significant as the markers of identity that would include race and region of birth or affiliation. In spatial terms, they also have a uniquely late-twentieth–early-twenty-first-century freedom of mobility—freedom to travel in a large world, not just "a trip to bountiful" or "a sudden trip home in the spring," but trips to Vermont or Massachusetts or Rhode Island, to Paris and the capitals of Europe, to Africa and through the African diaspora, to the Middle and Far East, and in each location to understand motion and travel itself as concomitant with their attitudinal stance in the world they inhabit. They belong wherever they are. Connected by e-mail, pager, cell phone, and additional almost unimaginable technology, they can be at home and at work anywhere, even on the road. In the fluidity of space, they forgo the insular and fuse meditations on social constructions with postmodern riffs on epistemology. And while they do indeed create visions of self and family, structures and institutions of family and identity, they worship at no altar of nuclear familial bonding. In fact, "Where are you from?" is as outmoded a question as "Who are your people?"

Two of these youngsters are central to my meditation on gliding into the next century: Shay Youngblood and Randall Kenan, both of whom published first books in 1989. They are central because read together their texts yield a series of repositionings that speak to the twenty-first century and their location within it as writers and new southerners.

A native of Columbus, Georgia, Shay Youngblood received a B.A. (1981) from Clark University, now Clark-Atlanta University, and an M.F.A. (1993) from Brown University. She is a playwright, screenplay writer, novelist, and so much more—a creative truth-sayer. She has, as the old people would say, "iron in her back." Youngblood was a Peace Corps volunteer in Dominica (1981), where, while serving as agricultural information officer, she wrote her first published short story, "In A House of Wooden Monkeys." She has been an au pair and an artist's model in Paris, work that informs her laundry list of survivalist jobs in her second novel, *Black Girl In Paris.* In addition to writing over the past two decades, she has been a teacher of creative writing and of black women's literature. She exemplifies the having-it-all and doing-it-all characteristic of her peers who have elected to write, who have studied writing in formal programs, and who expect to earn their living as writers. Hip, humorous, and "womanish," to use Alice Walker's apt term, Youngblood has already displayed excellent wordsmithing abilities, brave creative insights, and remarkably diverse energies, which together signify that she is and will be a formidable talent into the twenty-first century.

When *The Big Mama Stories* appeared from Firebrand Books, a radical feminist press in Ithaca, New York, it was a cause for celebration: a new southern black woman's voice raised in tribute to all her mamas and kin. Why was Firebrand's publishing Youngblood's stories so special? One reason was that the twelve narratives are rich with the sounds of a South quite familiar to a generation of readers, and the voices are resonant with the living, vibrant language of black folk speakers. Another reason, and "quiet as it's kept" (to use a phrase from Toni Morrison), Shay Youngblood has been truly significant, genuinely original in revolutionizing not simply what we now know and understand as contemporary black women's fiction but what we know and understand to be southern literature and African American literature. When few black women living in the present-day South were writing about the nitty-gritty issues impacting the lives of here and now African American women, matters of class, sexuality, extended family, and urban geography, Shay Youngblood was on the case. She has been a quiet storm of creative energy and vision and achievement.[6]

The Big Mama Stories, coming at the end of the 1980s, announced both a major, mature talent and a distinctive, fearless voice. Gendered large, the stories are the endruns on what is recurrent in Youngblood's novels: sexual exploitation and sexual violence, rape, abortion, class antagonism, homophobia, black revolution, urban development and cityscapes, new familial configurations, kin by choice not blood, matriarchy and patriarchy, lesbianism, reproduction and reproductive rights, spirituality, dreams and dream makers, and yes, love! all of which came under her steady gaze and filtered through her visionary fiction into our consciousness of racial, gender, class, and spatial diversity and our consciousness of the voices of ordinary people in today's extraordinary world. Not surprisingly, one of the stories, "Born with Religion," won a Pushcart Prize.

The decade of the 1990s was Shay Youngblood's decade of quiet fire: productions of her plays *Shakin' the Mess Outta Misery*, adapted from her stories (1988) and optioned by Sidney Poitier, and *Talking Bones*, winner of the Lorraine Hansberry Playwriting Award. She also wrote a screenplay of *Shakin'* for Columbia Pictures. Her play *Square Blues* was the Edward Albee honoree at the 21st Century Playwrights Festival and was selected by Anna Deavere Smith to receive a playwriting award from the Paul Green Foundation. Her plays also include *Black Power Barbie* and *Communism Killed My Dog*. Her story "In a House of Wooden Monkeys" was chosen by Gloria Naylor for her collection *Children of the Night: The Best Short Stories by Black Writers, 1967 to the Present;* and her first novel, *Soul Kiss*, was published to widespread critical acclaim for its lyrical intelligence, its confident subjectivity, its nuanced eroticism, and, not least, for its beautiful writing, its "exquisite, loving attention to language and story," as Tina

McElroy Ansa, another of the youngsters, so eloquently put it in a blurb for the novel.[7]

In the opening sentence of *Soul Kiss,* Youngblood sets a poetic tone for the entire text:

> The first evening Mama doesn't come back, I make a sandwich with leaves from her good-bye letter. I want to eat her words. I stare at the message written on the stiff yellowed paper as if the shaky scrawl would stand up and speak to me. *Mama loves you. Wait here for me.* I want her to take back the part about waiting. After crushing the paper into two small balls I flatten them with my fist, then stuff them into the envelope my aunt Faith gave me after Mama had gone. I feel weak as water and stone cold as I set with my legs dangling over the edge of the thick mattress on the high iron-frame bed, reading by the dim lamplight. (1–2)

Mariah's love for her mother is refracted through her love for words, taught to her by her mother, who devised word games to entertain and to bond with her daughter. Her mother, thus, arms Mariah for life with the gifts of orality and textuality. Because of its celebration of language as an intricate part of development and maturation, *Soul Kiss* is an extraordinary coming-of-age story that renders the complicated textures of late-twentieth-century lives, and it is a narration of transformative reality and beauty, those areas beyond the natural confines of complacency with things as they are or are supposed to be. "Alone in my room that night," Mariah ends her story, "I write down the last word my mother gave me. *Water.* I lift the edge of the paper to my lips and I drink it off the page, swallow it in two long syllables until it meets the place that is burning as brightly as day. . . . I am light as a page in a blank book. I feel empty but somehow whole. . . . The sun comes out and the grass is green again and the taste of water is sweet. I write poems and draw maps of language" (206).

Black Girl in Paris, Youngblood's second novel, has been praised for its portrait of a young female writer in the Paris of expatriate black writers, Wright and Baldwin in particular.[8] However, Eden, the twenty-six-year-old protagonist, is established as a particularly southern young woman, who is inspired to undertake her trip to Paris in part because of the existence of a buried and unfulfilled life working in a southern residence, Villa Luisa, the Dimple mansion, built by a black family with a fortune from their Plantation Restaurant, where black women dressed like Aunt Jemima and black men served in white uniforms. Villa Luisa has been turned into a museum, or a memorial to a dead man and, ultimately, to his unfulfilled dreams and loves. Eden's Aunt Vic, a woman free within herself who takes Eden "on the first Saturday morning of each month for blessings at the church of Modern Miracles," has urged her to seek the City of Light, where "black people are free. . . . Free to live where you wanted, work where you were qualified and love who you wanted. At least that was the rumor that she had heard." Eden, instead, takes classical voice lessons from "a mean old Creole woman who used to be an entertainer," and she dreams of Paris: "I made maps in my mind that would lead to other worlds." This is a way of breaking out of the linear and spatial organization of a regional literature. Indirectly, Paris becomes the point of possibility not yet available in the newly integrated but still racially problematical South.

Whereas Eden's literary forebears had to leave for Europe because of racial discrimination and racial oppression, she is not compelled to leave the country to become a writer. That she does so is, in part, owing to her sense of the way in which the careers of Wright and Baldwin took shape. "I needed a map to help me find love and language," she muses, "and since one didn't exist, I'd have to invent one following the trails and signs left by other travelers. I didn't know what I wanted to be but I knew I wanted to be the kind of woman who was bold, took chances and had adventures." In other words, a woman who could sashay across the City of Light and find her way. As museum guide, traveling companion, artist's model, *au pair*, poet's helper, lover, English teacher, thief (Eden's occupations in France that function as chapter titles), Eden works her map of adventures and becomes a witness and a writer. She has, however, already been a child singer-dancer in a juke joint:

> I would sing songs I heard on Aunt Vic's record player. Aunt Vic taught me how to lift the hem of my dress and dance at the end of the song like Josephine Baker and the French can-can dancers who looked so glamorous in the photographs she showed me. The audience would throw handfuls of change and crumbled dollar bills at my dancing feet. . . . If Mama hadn't found out when I was thirteen, I might have become a star on the dirt-floor circuit.

The landscape of the South has become something very different from what Wright represented in his fictions of rural Mississippi. It is not the space of incarceral mandates from a white power structure for unruly or improperly socialized blacks. It is instead a space that, while still circumscribed by the remnants of the past, is nonetheless open to the possibilities of black development. That space may well be aligned metaphorically with the South as a symbolic space for a new generation of writers. Youngblood's multiple talents, cross-genre interests, and thematic proclivities predict that into the next century she will most certainly be prominent in the rubric of "southern women writers."

Randall Kenan, although born in Brooklyn, New York, in 1963, was reared in Chinquapin, North Carolina. He studied fiction writing at the University of North Carolina, Chapel Hill, where he received a B.A. in English (1985). After a stint as an editorial assistant at the Alfred A. Knopf publishing house (1985–89), Kenan turned to teaching creative writing. Since 1989 he has held several prestigious appointments at Sarah Lawrence, Columbia, and Duke, where in 1994 he was the first William M. Blackburn Visiting Professor of creative writing; he was also the Edouard Morot-Sir Visiting Professor of creative writing at the University of North Carolina, Chapel Hill, in 1995, and the John and Renee Grisham Writer-in-Residence at the University of Mississippi, Oxford, in 1997, where he followed the previous Grisham Writers T. R. Pearson, Mark Richard, Mary Hood, and Tim Gautreaux. While in Oxford, he completed *Walking on Water* and worked on a new novel. Grove Press published his first novel, *A Visitation of Spirits*, in 1989, and Harcourt, Brace, his short-story collection *Let the Dead Bury Their Dead* in 1992.

Quiet as it's kept, Randall Kenan, too, has been revising conceptions of new southern fiction. He has been constructing a late twentieth-century southern and African American fiction that has antecedents in regionalized and racialized and gendered fiction from early Truman Capote to late Katherine Anne Porter, from Alice Walker to Richard Wright, from Carson McCullers and Flannery O'Connor to Ernest Gaines and James Alan McPherson. But, quiet as it's kept, Randall Kenan has also projected a twenty-first-century break with those writers and has freed his writing from the formal, thematic, and imagistic chains of traditional southern fiction and conventional African American fiction. Randall Kenan, for example, writes the coming-of-age narrative in a way that allows at once the shock of recognition and the unmistakable sense of the surprisingly new.

"Quiet as it's kept," the italicized phrase beginning his acknowledgments in *A Visitation of Spirits*, opens a space for positioning Kenan within the discursive practices of contemporary American and African American writing's most looming presence: "*Quiet as it's kept, a first novel is not written on a midnight candle and bread alone.*"[9] These words form his own intertextual homage to Nobel laureate Toni Morrison's first novel, *The Bluest Eye*. The second of two prologues demarking the contextual parameters of the text, Morrison's "Quiet as it's kept" is also an italicized interrogation of the production of narrative. The passage in her novel begins, "Quiet as it's kept, there were no marigolds in the fall of 1941. We thought, at the time, that it was Pecola was having her father's baby that the marigolds did not grow." After two richly evocative and dense paragraphs, the passage ends in a two-sentence paragraph: "There is really nothing more to say—except why. But since why is difficult to handle, one must take refuge in how." The "how" then becomes the subject of Morrison's narrative, how Pecola's young life ended in madness, stunted growth like the marigold seeds that would not grow in 1941, and the "how" necessarily allows for an epigrammatical yet time-obsessed narration of individual life stories, familial and social history, and racial memory. But the words, "Quiet as it's kept," remain the signifier of both narrative voice and communal agency in all of their multiplicity.[10]

Those very words, however, and their referent in Morrison and Kenan could not have any more different implications than if they were initiating a conversation between earth and Mars or Venus. Yet, at the same time, the two narratives converge in the conception of the linkages between identity and difference, between subjectivity and sexuality, between communal expectations determined by history, memory, and the culture and individual dreams fueled by desires, commodities, and textuality. Morrison's trope of the failed growth of marigold seeds, with an empathetic link to Pecola and her stunted growth, becomes transfigured in Kenan's trope of "plant tropism," as Horace Cross names the project he and Gideon Stone collaborate on for their science project: "It's the study of what makes plants grow the way they do" (151); "an orientation of an organism, usually by growth rather than by movement, in response to an external stimulus" (155).

In their narratives of the thwarted maturation of youth racialized as black and gendered female (Morrison's Pecola) and gendered male (Kenan's Horace), marginalized by the customs and conventions of place or space as much as by race and gender, the two texts speak to the self/other enactment of power relations and interrogate a search, whether linear or circular, for identity that would have as the expected outcome an authentic, essential core that is hidden to consciousness. Such projects are rejected by Kenan in his representation of Horace Thomas Cross, a protagonist struggling to understand why and how he has grown in a particular way, one at odds with his rural religious community but not so different from the pattern of growth implicit but suppressed in men and family members beloved in that community.

Trinh T. Minh-ha, in "Not You/Like You: Postcolonial Women and the Interlocking Questions of Identity and Difference," states: "If identity refers to the whole pattern of sameness within a being, the style of a continuing me that permeates all the changes undergone, then difference remains within the boundary of that which distinguishes one identity from another."[11] Her point is that difference should not be excluded from the process of identity formation or of marking the distinctiveness of identity. In *A Visitation of Spirits*, Kenan undertakes just such a project, one in which Horace's subjectivity is articulated through his seeking to understand his difference, his identity as "a by-product of a manhandling of life," to use Trinh T. Minh-ha's formulation of difference that very often lands an individual "in a hospital, a rehabilitation center, a concentration camp, or a reservation" (415). In Horace's case, it produces madness and death.

With the five chapter titles, "White Sorcery," "Black Necromancy," "Holy Science," "Old Demonology," and "Old Gods, New Demons," Kenan represents the occult, black and white magic, and ancient properties all together, all aligned with the contradictory sameness and otherness of Horace Cross, the protagonist, and his cousin, the theologian, preacher, teacher, first black principal of an integrated school in his county, and writer of sermons and playlike dialogues, James Malachai Greene, whose meditations form the backdrop for interrogating Horace's death:

It's as if I'm trying to write the sermon I want to hear, not the perfect sermon, but the perfect sermon for me.

So I pore over the Bible, reading, taking notes, making tentative outlines. Banishing from my mind any thoughts of the present, of the recent past, of the uncertain future. Thinking only of God and his laws. (38)

In many ways, Cousin Jimmy's, that is, James Malachai Greene's, meditative voice forms the contrapuntal access to both explorations of the Tims Creek community and of the demon complicating and truncating Horace's young life. Linked in their overt characteristics, Horace and Jimmy are also linked in the buried sexuality each seeks to suppress: "Horace . . . Lord, he was like this here Jimmy. Quiet. Polite. There ain't nothing wrong with quiet. . . . But this was a difference" (55).

The text, however, while epigraphically playing off Charles Dickens's *Christmas Carol* and Scrooge's question, "Are spirits' lives so short?" calls up and defines its demon against a second epigraph, William Gibson's observation in *Neuromancer:* "To call up a demon you must learn its name. Men dreamed that, once, but now it is real in another way. . . ." Noticeably both epigraphs invoke spirits and demons, but importantly, they also call up time and the imperative of the present, the moment, the now: "To-night at midnight. Hark! The time is drawing near" (Dickens) and "Men dreamed that, once, but now it is real in another way" (Gibson). The conceptualization of time boundaries anticipates the Scripture and Biblical references to the House of the Lord, as the challenged and contested site of knowledge and action within the present moment. Religion, myth, and demonology all intermingle in a James Baldwinesque fantasia of spiritual possession and homoerotics in Kenan's text.

Indeed, *A Visitation of Spirits* is a "coming out" novel, a narrative of transfiguration perhaps, told with the vision and the eloquence of a seer and sayer. Yet, this novel's honesty about sexuality, about homosexuality, is not something that southern literature of the renaissance could or would represent. Truman Capote's exquisite *Other*

Voices, Other Rooms left no immediate progeny. It is rarely something that African American literature before the late 1980s represented except in homoerotic implicated situations and relational identities.[12] James Baldwin's *Another Country* was a lone signifier of such relationships and their complex consequences. In *A Visitation of Spirits*, it is as though the gender roles compelling a heterosexual erotics also constricted the fiction to fantasies of masculinity devoid of sex and imbued with character traits that ignore the physical body. Here Kenan takes to the next level what we have seen in such late-twentieth-century fiction.

The first section of *A Visitation of Spirits*, "White Sorcery," bears the epigraph: "The Lord is in his Holy Temple; / let all the earth keep silent before him. / I was glad when they said unto me, Let us go into the House of the Lord. . . ." "White Sorcery" begins with time: "December 8, 1985 8:45 A.M." and the words of ninety-two-year-old Aunt Ruth, "Lord, Lord, Lord . . ." (3). The pressure of time and the omnipresence of Christianity within the community establish the parameters of the text and of Horace's search for a space within both to develop and to be himself. "Advent (or The Beginning of the End)" begins the brief subsegment "December 8, 1985," of "White Sorcery" (6) and establishes the developmental space as North Carolina, a rural farming country, and emphasizes hog killing as a ritual of the area and its people, in particular the allowing of a boy to aim, fire a gun into the hog as part of an initiation into the local customs of masculinity and power. The gun as a symbol both of maturation, domination, and destruction recurs throughout the text as a naked Horace makes his way in a night world toward death.[13]

The second dated section of "White Sorcery," "April 29, 1984 11:30 A.M." (11) occurs a year earlier than the first and produces Horace as subject by means of textuality—books, papers, pictures and images from books, reference texts, scientific books (18), and ancient or invented and fictionalized rituals (21–22). It is also marked by intertextuality specifically linking "White Sorcery" with texts by Charles

Chesnutt, a writer from the same section of southeastern North Carolina who concerned himself with the transformative implicit in the fluidity of racial identity in his novels of passing, such as *The House Behind the Cedars* (1900) and the posthumously published *Paul·Marchand, Free Man of Color* (1999), and in his stories of conjuring, *The Conjure Woman and Other Tales* (1899), with their racially and politically informed oppositional narrative stances. Chesnutt's turn-of-the-nineteenth-into-the-twentieth-century narratives seem appropriate for projecting Kenan's work as *fin de siècle* and twenty-first-century writing.

The question opening "April 29, 1984," is suspended *in medias res:* " . . . What to become?" Dislocated from the time and people of the preceding section but refining the place descriptives ("swampy woodlands of Southeastern North Carolina" [11], with "Wilmington, Kinston, Goldsboro" as the nearest large towns, [18]) the section answers the question by presenting Horace Thomas Cross, "the Great Black Hope," at sixteen. His becoming is the transfiguration at the center of the text—a transfiguration resonant of the transformation of a sequence of animals: rabbit, fox, hawk, squirrels, mice, wood rats, snakes, dogs, butterflies, cats, and finally a bird. The transformation of humans into animals and vice versa marking fairy tales and myths figures centrally in Horace's narrative. Horace concludes, "There are no moral laws that say: You must remain human. And he would not" (12). The tale that links transformation and vision is one of the most compelling; in it old Julia turns herself into an eel on the bottom of the ocean "to see what she could see." Horace's own choice is of a red-tailed hawk for his transfiguration (14–15). Horace is seeking a way out; he links himself to Daniel, Isaac, and the woman at the well—all Biblical seekers and believers. At the same time, his room is papered with pictures of sorcerers, conjurers, magicians, Wonder Woman, heroic action figures, Batman (17). The descriptions of his conjuring, burning the dead kitten and incanting the demon (21–22), returning to the woods in the midnight hour and chanting (25–

26), taking his grandfather's gun and following a voice, one voice, the voice (27–28), are integral to the descriptions of fornication and violence and danger, which taken together signify homoeroticism linked with dread and transfiguration (28).

The second part of the novel, "Black Necromancy," bears the epigraph "Whosoever will let him come. . . ." (29) and contains "James Malachai Greene Confessions," the Jimmy of the opening segment. He is a preacher-educator whose relationship with Philip Schnider, one of his professors at a seminary, a Jew who converted to Christianity, centers on theology as a desire to know God (33). He connects himself to Horace (36) as having curiosity and begins the process of "contemplating the equation of eternal life. Why? How?" (36) Knowledge, like memory and mourning, catalyzes the narrative reflections. The play scenario, set on 30 April 1984 (40–43), one day after Horace's death, and culminating with Jimmy's acknowledgment of the horror that his cousin Horace is possessed by a demon (43), provides access to the mystery of Jimmy's own existence and his relation to both his God and his family. It become apparent that Kenan is thinking through what he calls "the emotional aspect of being black or white—a true ghost of the mind, the thing Americans will be trying to exorcize for a long time to come." Horace's possession has as much to do with race as it does with sexuality and religion. As a young, gay black youth, Horace has no models and no mentors to steer him away from schizophrenia and self-destruction.

After the horrific narrative of Horace Thomas Cross's confessions, the final section of the novel begins "A Requiem for Tobacco," a lament for that which is dead, times that are past: "You remember, though perhaps you don't, that once upon a time men harvested tobacco by hand. There was a time when folk were bound together in a community, as one, and helped one person this day and that day another. . . . But this was once upon a time" (254). The emphasis on memory and the repetition of time, "once upon a time," "There was a time," and "this was once upon a time," serve at once to mythologize the concept of the harvest and to foreclose the narrative interrogation of harvest. The impulse is to hold on to the memory of harvesting tobacco by hand because too many have no memory, yet the memory is itself curiously at odds with Horace's own development and death, for it cannot contain the homosexual desire and consequences that charge the larger text. "It is good to remember, for too many forget" (257); the concluding words may speak to the now lost tobacco culture, but they also evoke the Horace who is also lost to the terms, religious and sexual, of that culture. The requiem in its largest implications also becomes a societal lament for a familiar but now vacant and lost southern rural culture, but there is no hint of nostalgia for its return. It is better off, Kenan implies, dead, good, and gone.

Death, past, and loss in human and communal terms are reiterated in Kenan's second book, *Let the Dead Bury Their Dead* (1992), a collection of short stories nominated for the National Book Critics Circle Award in Fiction that was also a *New York Times* Notable Book of 1992. The book received the 1994 Whiting Award and its prize of thirty thousand dollars, given annually to "writers of exceptional talent and promise." From magical children who speak to the dead, to praying hogs, to brother-sister incest, to gay lovers going South to bury their dead and meeting the conventional families who do not know that men live together as husband and wife, to a Maroon Society near Tims Creek, the fictional community recurring in his fiction—in all this Kenan produces a South and a southern past that has little to do with Faulkner's Yoknapatawpha or Gaines's Bayonne and everything to do with the kind of creation that marked those earlier fictionists.

Kenan is a fabulist, who calls up a past that is an in-your-face reminder of what has been left out of southern storytelling. His take on male sexuality is complex and compassionate. A grieving grandmother, for instance, comes to terms with her dead grandson's life as a gay man when his lover, who is both from another region and of a different race, visits her. Yet Kenan's unflinching attention to same-sex relationships does not mean that he sees himself "as a voice for gay rights," but rather as a southern writer, one aware of the necessity of change: "David Leavitt's *Family Dancing* broke some important barriers in the early '80s for treating homosexual relations in fiction. I see myself trying to break some of those same barriers in the South in a way similar to that of writers like Rita Mae Brown."[14]

In his stories, Kenan blends the impossible with the practical and the known. For instance, in the title story, "Let the Dead Bury Their Dead," he weaves a magical tale of a group of maroons in North Carolina and documents the fact-fantasy with historical footnotes that project a not-to-be-doubted reality onto the page. The notes supply as much text as the narrative itself. Like Caryl Phillips or David Bradley, Randall Kenan, in the story of maroons, moves to collapse the difference between fact, fiction, history, and memory. In an interview for *Book Page*, he explains that the seemingly "found history" detailing the origins of Tims Creek "started inside *A Visitation of Spirits*, but got too out of hand," so he began another strategy, "playing with the melding of fiction and fact which was not central to the story line of the novel." What he arrived at in the long title story was an interweaving of fact and fiction that, he has suggested, "pulls together what I am trying to create in the book. It underscores how all fiction is lies and hopefully a lot more." And like a master word sorcerer and magician, he succeeds in inventing a new image of the South. It is no wonder that Terry McMillan has called him our black Márquez.

There is, of course, much more to be said of Randall Kenan's fiction and of Shay Youngblood's. However, here I consider only what they and their fiction may be telling us about southern writing in the twenty-first century.

IV. Chassé

There are at least six clearly readable and relevant points in the award-winning writings of Shay Youngblood and Randall Kenan that place them within a diagnostic loop relating to new southern writing.

These points are not intended, however, to create a metanarrative truncating discourses on their work.

1. They are independent of southern restrictive covenants in both their subject matter and their subjectivities. Shay Youngblood has said: "I am interested in transformation, sparked by generational influence, how traditions are passed on in different cultures, how an individual's actions can create global, political, and social changes. I write as a call to action, using theatre as a verb." She is well aware of how her own writing may generate change. Randall Kenan understands how his writing functions to reshape power relations. His work as a black southern writer challenges both racial hierarchies and racial dominance so that a different power dynamic may result.

2. They are cosmopolitan and live in a wide world not circumscribed by old practices and expectations. They are free to travel within space as much as within time, as did previous generations whose looks backward took them into explorations of the experiences of the past. Youngblood's *Soul Kiss,* for example, begins on a military base in Kansas, relocates to a town in Georgia, and after a bus trip across the United States to Los Angeles takes in multiethnic California before concluding back in Georgia. Randall Kenan traveled the United States researching and talking to people for his book *Walking on Water: Black American Lives at the Turn of the Twenty-first Century* (Knopf, 1999). Within the geographic spaciousness that they occupy, Kenan and Youngblood project a linguistic expansiveness and produce voices that are not trapped within the old linguistic codes and verbal patterns. Mariah in *Soul Kiss* recognizes as much:

I check out diction tapes from the library and practice speaking out loud to erase my southern accent so when I raise my hand to speak in class my teachers will understand me. I play my cello. . . . Rosemary [the cello] is a big comfort to me in all the hours I spend alone. We make sounds that massage my lungs, my heart, the insides of my thighs. I miss the poetry of southern words in my mouth so I plant a few in the ficus tree and water them tenderly . . . *yonder ways . . . sweet potato pie . . . cut the monkey . . .* and always I plant *sweet . . . blue . . . music . . . Mama.* Soon the plant begins to grow, a bit sideways and very slowly, but I see growth and all the words I love in each green veined leaf. (128)

3. They are open to frank discourses of sexuality alongside race or gender or class as a marker of identity and as a category of analysis. Erotic, humorous, and tragic yet sassily outrageous in the matter of sexual experience, Kenan and Youngblood push the limits of hetero- sexual social mandates. In his stories, such as "Cornsilk," in which he portrays the end of an incestuous affair, or "The Foundations of the Earth," in which he explores the conflict between Christianity and homosexuality, as in his novel, Kenan displays a willingness to treat human sexuality in all its manifestations and in terms of a dis- position toward psychoanalytic interpretation. And, importantly, he does so with enormous compassion and sensitivity rather than with voyeurism or sensationalism.

Youngblood explores homoerotic desire and the discovery of its unarticulated boundaries when she writes about sibling incest be- tween sisters in "Funny Women" and the erotic attraction between young girls, between mother and daughter, or between father and daughter in *Soul Kiss,* yet she explodes the notion of deviant sex- ual behavior by normalizing her protagonist's dressing in her father's clothes while masturbating to his pornography as actions of utter loneliness and aloneness, not of sexual desire. The point, however, is not to shock or incite, but rather to consider the erotic as a factor in the maturation and development of social beings and social relations. For instance, as a young girl Mariah names her cello Rosemary, and the music she makes becomes an extension of her body as well as of her interconnectedness with people.

4. They are no longer focused on the black-white binary of south- ern race relations. Randall Kenan, writing in *Brightleaf* (Fall 1998),

puts it this way: "Already I had rejected . . . race as a biological reality, but I could not ignore how the concept preyed on the modern mind—how the concept of race still informed the way black folk and white folk interacted. So whether race existed or not, it was not a moot point." In an extended commentary, he goes on to paint the iconic details supporting his view:

> Culturally speaking blackness is both a chimera and an angel of change. It is hard to pin down because it is ever changing and belongs to everyone who has a back strong enough to seek it out and be true to it. Anthropologists can tell us what black Americans retain from the Ibo or from the Yoruba, but when my nieces dance to the music of Missy Elliot, it is not Ghana they dream of, but [of] their present-day American Dreamscape: Wal-Marts and Chevy trucks, McDonalds value meals and Walt Disney, chicken fajitas and Eddie Bauer swimwear. Once that culture was defined by the church, the Bible, certain landscapes, and certain shared experiences of people segregated and physically excluded from the larger society. But that America vanished with World War II, the Civil Rights Act, radio, interstates and Black Entertainment Television.

The racial designations in Youngblood's *Soul Kiss* are equally multiple, mixed, and permeable. Mariah Santos has a Cherokee great-grandfather, and her last name suggests Hispanic heritage, as does the Spanish language she and her mother sprinkle through their speech and thoughts. Her black classmates in Georgia tease her: "And with a stupid name like Mariah Santos you must be Mexican or something" (45). Her Japanese American teacher in Los Angeles is Mrs. Oyama, whose mother is a black poet from North Carolina and whose father is a Japanese journalist from outside of Tokyo; they have been married forty-five years. Her friends are Mexican, East Indian, Korean, and "a blue-eyed boy from Arkansas." Her world is not race coded in the old ways. Eden, the protagonist of *Black Girl in Paris*, is a slant-eyed orphan, whose blackness is already complicated by her location outside a racially defined community; in effect, nationality rather than race becomes the primary marker positioning Eden in relation to the French and the expatriates she meets in Paris. Moreover, unlike southern writers on race of earlier generations, Youngblood and Kenan are not seeking to validate or shape a racial identity in their texts; instead, they assume one and glide on. As Kenan has put it in "Whose Race Is It Anyway?" "If it isn't a biological reality, why can't we throw the idea away?" when he imagines African American identity "as composed of a number of disparate elements, among them and most pronounced politics, culture, and emotion."

In a similar vein, in her prizewinning story "Born with Religion," Youngblood, for example, describes a group of elderly black women in the #2 mission prayer circle meeting who come together to pray over one of their members:

> Aunt Mae, Big Mama's other sister, didn't come cause she said she wasn't a member of no church and besides she always went to the dog races over in Alabama on Tuesday nights. Said she would pray where she wanted to, but she would pray.
>
> Miss Mary always showed up first. She looked like a skinny black gypsy. She had six gold-teeth right in front, wore big gold earrings and bright-colored scarves over her finger-length plaits that stuck out from under. Then came Miss Alice a light-skinned sister with the bluest eyes and hair I'd ever seen. Then Miss Tom came in. She was a mannish-looking woman with a mustache. She took the neighborhood kids fishing every summer. Then Miss Emma Lou comes in, short, dark and bowlegged, still wearing her white maid's uniform and carrying a spit cup. The woman didn't go nowhere without a tin of sweet Georgia Peach snuff in her apron pocket. . . . And late as always came Miss Lamama. Her real name was Jessie Pearl Lumumba. At 17 she married an African and took to wearing African dresses and took on African-like ways. [15]

Raced, gendered, but not your usual cast of characters, these women form a carefully constructed family.

5. They articulate new family configurations. Matisse, Mariah's father, is Joe El Jr., a painter who never married her mother but who loves her long after their several intense weeks together end. Coral, Mariah's mother, a nurse, leaves her daughter with her relatives in Georgia and never returns for her, but her quirky maternal nurturing gives her daughter a tactile, aural, visual, and oral facility that stamps her life and makes her amazingly resistant to destruction. Eden, in Youngblood's *Black Girl in Paris,* is an orphan—a found baby adopted by a loving, childless couple, an ordinary working-class couple who choose adoption because of the abandoned baby's needs and not because of their own.

6. They collapse the rigidity of forms and experiment with collages of formal techniques. While Youngblood uses the artifacts (visas, stamps, metro tickets, etc.) from an actual sojourn in Paris to mark the material culture of her subject and to divide her fiction into sections, Kenan, in particular, exemplifies the experimentation and fluidity of forms characteristic of much recent writing. Stylistically, Kenan's novel *A Visitation of Spirits* is elegant, daring, and sophisticated; traditional storytelling techniques are absent and replaced by stream of conscious voices from the grave, spirits bound to remembering the past and to telling visions that produce tableaux of personal memory and communal history and transfiguration. It sashays across time and space, living and dead, with an indulgent wonder at the possibilities and potential of freedom in form. It is a metafictional text in terms of orality (the writer can die before he can write his narrative but even in death can speak its truth) and playwriting (the performativity of the stylistic device of the play format).[16] It is a text steeped in blood, killing, death, ghosts, and bodies; corporeal images that both transfix and transform.

These, then, are the prominent, observable aspects of Youngblood and Kenan speaking as twenty-first-century southern writers. What they are saying is predicated upon their clear-sighted engagement with the craft of writing and the interrogation of what it means to write from an intersectional subject position. And if anyone cares to check them out on the web, it will be immediately apparent that they are enjoying their vocation—no tortured, conflicted artists here, not if their interviews and websites are any indication of their experiential realities or the prospects for their futures.

NOTES

1. Both definitions are adapted from *The American Heritage Dictionary.*

2. C. Hugh Holman, "No More Monoliths, Please: Continuities in the Multi-Souths," in *Southern Literature in Transition: Heritage and Promise*, ed. Philip Castille and William Osborne (Memphis: Memphis State University Press, 1983), xviii.

3. Holman, *Southern Literature,* xix. Holman's listing of Ellison, Wright, Gaines, and Reed is a progressive step forward from racial exclusiveness, but his inclusion of four black men recalls the ideology that inspired *But Some of Us Are Brave: Black Women's Studies.* The first full title was *All the Women Are White, All the Blacks Are Men, But Some of Us Are Brave.*

4. Larry Griffin, "Southern Distinctiveness, Yet Again, or, Why America Still Needs the South," *Southern Cultures* 6 (fall 2000): 47–72.

5. Though *Abiding Appalachia* (San Diego: Harcourt Brace Jovanovich, 1978; 1994) first appeared in 1978, recognition for its author came slowly. A decade later, Awiakta received the 1989 Distinguished Tennessee Writers Award, and in 1991 she won the Award for Outstanding Contribution to Appalachian Literature.

6. The term "quiet storm" is now applied to radio music shows that follow the programming format and style of Howard University's pioneering jazz show "Quiet Storm."

7. Shay Youngblood, *Soul Kiss* (New York: Riverhead Books, 1997). Hereafter cited in text.

8. Shay Youngblood, *Black Girl in Paris* (New York: Riverhead Books, 2000).

9. Randall Kenan, *A Visitation of Spirits: A Novel* (New York: Anchor Books, 1989).

10. Toni Morrison, *The Bluest Eye* (New York: Knopf, 1993).

11. Trinh T. Minh-ha, "Not You/Like You: Postcolonial Women and the Interlocking Questions of Identity and Difference," in *Dangerous Liaisons: Gender, Nation, and Postcolonial Perspectives*, ed. Anne McClintock, Aamire Mufti, and Ella Shohat (University of Minnesota Press, 1997), 415.

12. Readers may wish to refer to the attraction-repulsion between Trueblood and Norton in Ralph Ellison's *Invisible Man*, which may also be figured as homoerotic as well as a voyeuristic exploration of desire and father-daughter incest.

13. Kenan, *A Visitation of Spirits,* 7–9; see also the final meditation on hogs and time past, 9–10.

14. Randall Kenan, "Meet Randall Kenan: Southern Writing Is Changing, It Has to Change," interview by H. B. Grace, *Book Page* (April 1992). Kenan refers to Rita Mae Brown's 1973 novel *Rubyfruit Jungle*, a narrative tracing the coming out of Molly Bolt, a young southern feminist.

15. Shay Youngblood, "Born with Religion," in *The Big Mama Stories* (Ithaca: Firebrand Books, 1989), 14.

16. Kenan, *A Visitation of Spirits.* See especially 40–43, 110–14, and 181–88.

The Inevitable Future of the South

EDWARD L. AYERS

Journal: October 21, 2076
Assignment for history for Monday: trace the origins of the contemporary South.

Note to self: I'm wearing my infoglasses, of course, scanning the archive and narrating these notes. Got some good music shaking the background. I'll give some facts, quotes, pictures, and sound that I can work into my presentation for tomorrow. The historical stuff from the late twentieth century looks funny, being in 2-D and all, but I can still make it out OK thanks to the Turner Enhancements that spruce it up.

I wouldn't say this out loud or anything, but this is kind of interesting. You know, growing up in Georgia, the capital of the Consolidated South, you hear this stuff all the time and kind of turn it off, but somehow it's clicking today. I guess that when you get to be sixteen you start seeing things in, like, perspective.

OK, my notes: All the footage and photos paint a pretty clear picture of things around 1950 or so. Back then the South was full of small places: small towns, small churches, small farms, small populations, small ambitions, small memories, small entertainment, small government. Some people even said they *liked* all that old stuff. I guess you can get used to anything.

But even then, now that we know what happened, you can see consolidation beginning. It all looks inevitable once you know how it turned out. In fact, I'm going to title this "The Inevitable Future of the South" because it's obvious to me that by 2000 things were pretty much lined up so that this had to happen as it did. We're always taught that 2043 is the key date, when the states surrendered most of their powers, and the Consolidation Agreement was signed, but it turns out that stuff had been going on a long time.

In some ways, the Consolidation started all the way back in the big war they had in the middle of the twentieth century, when the South was still way behind the rest of the country—behind even the ridiculously cold parts up north and the ridiculously dry parts out west. They had to build big army bases and big ships for the war, so they moved some of that to the South and paid people more than southerners had ever earned before. Cities grew real fast, and people got new cars and houses and things when the war ended, but the government and businesses kept spending.

But things were weird, because back then some people believed that people who had different skin colors were different *inside* too! Back before they could manipulate DNA so easily, they didn't realize that people are like 99.999 percent the same all over the world, all the way down to the genes and chromosomes. Although they could see that people they called "black" and "white" were in fact all different kinds of colors, that didn't stop them from lumping people together in two big groups. There had been all that slavery and stuff back in the ancient days and people just couldn't let it go, I guess.

What in the world would they have made of me, with my genealogy from Scotland, Ghana, Honduras, Korea, and the Cherokee Nation! I think that everybody would have felt differently back then if they had had the machinery that traced people's DNA twelve generations back like we do for our birth certificates. They would have seen that we're all in this together and have been for a long time.

Anyway, the South began to change around the middle of the twentieth century. They built the interstates, which were cool even if they did waste them on those evil vehicles that actually ran on petroleum, no matter how unlikely that sounds. Some people say that the first interstates were the true roots—and routes, ha-ha—of the Great Consolidation. It was along those interstates that the first spores of the Consolidation were planted: Exxons, McDonalds, Hardees, and all those other old-fashioned places that you see in the paintings in houses that are trying to create that old-timey feel. We can see from the time-lapse maps how those spores spread wherever the interstates crossed the old-fashioned roads into towns and cities, spreading those franchises into the country.

People began to get it, the basic idea behind the Great Consolidation: it was *good* to have everything you needed, just when you needed it, in the way you wanted it, the way you knew it would be. Back before then, you had very little control over your life. You had to eat different kinds of stuff because there were still nonstandardized restaurants around, places that didn't even belong to a franchise. You had to watch whatever they put on TV when they put it on. You had to travel to different places to get different experiences. Boy, it was lame.

So, while all this was going on, starting slow and kind of sputtering back in the 1950s and 1960s, something really big happened. And you know what it was: the Great Freedom, the big turning point in southern history. All the great men and women of the South— Parks, King, Marshall, and the other people on our money—led the revolution that got rid of that segregation junk. It was dangerous to fight against that skin-color craziness for a long time, and people kept trying to hold on to it for decades afterward in a sort of guerrilla warfare in schools and subdivisions and the like, but things had turned a corner.

Even the most selfish people eventually came to see that the Great Freedom freed the whole South, even the selfish people themselves. Business boomed very soon thereafter, and things began to take off almost as soon as the government quit spending its energy dividing people from one another. People from the cold part and the dry part of the country began to see what they should have seen all along: the South was the best place to live.

Check out these old clippings from around 2000, when people began to understand what was going on. I should be able to work these into my paper somewhere:

"Since 1978, the population of the South has risen by more than 20 million. The region's population growth rate—30%—is nearly double that of the rest of the nation."[1]

"Well-educated and affluent Americans are swelling the population of the South. . . . The influx, 90 percent white, is making the region better-educated and more affluent."[2]

During the 1990s, Florida, Georgia, and Texas have seen the largest influx of black professionals in the country, with North Carolina fifth. They are moving into integrated suburbs, especially in the newer cities of the South.[3]

"Since 1978, nearly four of every ten jobs gained in United States are in the South."[4]

"The I-85 corridor, as it runs through upstate South Carolina, is sometimes called America's autobahn. More than 90 international companies have located facilities in this growing metropolitan region. . . . Near the end of the 1990s, almost 2 million Southerners worked in foreign owned firms."[5]

"A thousand Japanese companies have located in the Southeast in the last 25 years, creating 140,000 jobs. That represents $26.5 billion investment in manufacturing."[6]

It wasn't just money from abroad that came to the South. A lot of companies from Germany and Japan sent workers to the South, and they decided to stay here. Also, a lot of other immigrants came to the South looking for some of the new jobs.

The South had been a pretty homogenous place for a long time, filled with people who considered themselves "white" or "black." But when all this development came the population changed too.

With its border with Mexico, Texas had a lot of Mexican immigrants for a long time; and being close to Cuba (back when that was its own country), Florida had a lot of Hispanic immigrants for a long time. But late in the century other places in the South got in on the act. Listen to this:

"A 1998 report shows that the top six Hispanic-growth counties are all in the South—two in the Atlanta area, two in urban North Carolina, one in the Virginia suburbs, and one in Arkansas."[7]

People from parts of Asia also began to gather in southern cities, and the South became, over the next fifty years or so, one of the most diverse parts of the United States.

The immigrants were much younger than the natives, either black or white. Young adult white people steadily became a smaller and smaller part of the population, while older white people, especially women, became a larger and larger part.

So you had a sort of volatile situation there, we see looking back.

A lot of these people came to cities, which suddenly got a lot bigger, because "of the 17.7 million jobs that the South has gained since 1978, metro areas accounted for fully 15 million."[8]

Four of the five cities that topped 500,000 during the 1990s were in the South: Austin, Charlotte, Nashville, and Fort Worth.[9]

That's when the capital of the Consolidated South really took off— good old Atlanta, where I kind of live. It exploded, man! Even though there was no really good reason for Atlanta to be where it was— since it didn't have a port or even a decent river or pretty mountains or anything like that—with its airport and highways it somehow managed to become THE place.

They built the whole darned thing around those infernal combustion cars, and the costs of that became clear pretty quickly. Here are some facts from 2000:

"Eight of the 20 cities most affected by sprawl are in the Southeast; Atlanta is first, with Washington, D.C., and Ft. Lauderdale not far behind."[10]

In Atlanta, approximately five hundred acres of open space are converted into subdivisions and shopping centers each week—"arguably the fastest rate of growth of any metropolitan region in human history."[11]

"People in Atlanta drive more miles each year . . . and more miles per person each day (34 miles) than anywhere else in the country." Drivers in Atlanta lost 133 million hours stuck in traffic.[12]

The only place worse than Atlanta back then was northern Virginia, the area around the old capital in Washington, D.C.

"Washington now has more folks working at information-technology companies than in the government," a reporter wrote back in 2000. "Near Vienna, the mega-office complex of Tyson's Corner—in the '50s, nothing more than a general store and a gas station—has more office space than all of downtown Washington. Virginia's Fairfax County is now the nation's richest."

All this grew up around Dulles Airport—built out in the middle of nowhere in the 1950s—and the conversion of the defense industry to what were called back then "computers" and the development of what they called "the Internet" back when that was a thing distinguishable from everything else.

The Inevitable Future of the South   93

The guy who wrote this tried to predict what would happen from this development, as if people had a clue back then what would happen. If this growth continues, he said, "It's possible that in one hundred years students of history will regard the Civil War and today's digital revolution as the region's most defining moments. Robert E. Lee? Steve Case? Could be."[13]

I don't think so, bud. Who the heck is Steve Case? Oh, I see: he started this company called America Online. He vanished without a trace because all these changes turned out to be a lot bigger than one guy or company. There have been dozens of Steve Cases since 2000. They come and go. Only the Consolidation endures. (Though, I must say, as I look over that America Online thing in the archives, it was a real step toward consolidation itself, turning the entire Internet into a kind of franchise. A brilliant move.)

Once the Consolidation started, it was hard to stop. The cities began to blend into one another, their suburbs overlapping and interconnecting. It was like some organism growing, growing, feeding on cars and prosperity and the hunger for a nice yard. The satellite movies clearly show it happening—and darned fast.

About ten years ago, of course, people decided to quit fighting it and went ahead and incorporated the biggest city in the world: Washingham, the crescent that runs from northern Virginia down to Birmingham. The spine that connects it all used to be interstate highways, where all the original consolidation grew up, but now, of course, that is all devoted to levitation corridors. I've not been to the whole city, but, fortunately, if you've seen one part of it you've seen a lot of it. That's the point, really, of consolidation.

Some people worried about the effects of all this growth. As early as

1998, more southerners than nonsoutherners said they "always feel rushed for time."[14]

People also noticed that "the country's divorce rate bulges the most at the Bible Belt. From the land of family values and Baptist preachers, 8 Deep South states rank in the Top 20 when it comes to divorce."[15]

A lot of the countryside was in trouble by this time. The counties up in the mountains, where they actually used to dig rocks out of the ground to burn for energy, were hit hard, but so were lots of other places that were off the interstates, that had weak schools, and that didn't have any cities nearby. Those places got pretty desperate while other places not far away got rich.[16]

Some counties got in such bad shape that they actually built their economies around importing trash and toxic waste from other states. When the climate warming that people had been warning of for a long time finally began, things began to flood and rot. One scary picture from 1999 shows something hard to believe: hurricanes flooded eastern North Carolina, "washing drowned hogs by the thousands down the state's once pristine streams." Gross, huh?[17]

In fact, the countryside in general got in worse and worse shape. You can see why. Back then people lived scattered all over the place. They chopped up the countryside into tiny little lots and farms, crisscrossed with fences, walls, roads, and such. People somehow believed it was healthier, better, to live isolated like that, to use up all the land for these minuscule places and to drive back and forth to it. It's a wonder people could feed themselves back then.

Fortunately, things began to change as the countryside got consolidated too. Almost all the good jobs appeared in the cities, and there was very little that people out in the country could do about it. Their schools began to decline, and their political power went too. Young people didn't want to try to scratch a living out of the farms they inherited, especially when they could sell the farms to people who wanted to extend the suburbs.

A pretty amazing change took place:

"In the 1960's . . . 10 percent still worked in agriculture. During the next decade, the farm population declined by another 50 percent. . . . By the mid 1990's, farmers composed only 2 percent of the southern population."[18]

This was when some very useful people came along, people who wanted to make really efficient farms, where they could produce what all those new people in the South needed to eat. They built larger and larger agricultural units, and they built better and better animals. Scientists cooked up improved cattle, pigs, turkeys, and chickens. They invented ways to grow catfish really quickly and harvest them really efficiently.

Here's what they did with chickens: They built "carefully designed confinement facilities, which housed each bird in an individual compartment, automatically delivered feed, water, and antibiotics in precisely measured amounts at optimal time intervals." They created chickens that gained three pounds in eight weeks on less than six pounds of feed.[19]

We can do a lot better now, of course, with the brainless chickens, and I feel a lot better about eating something that never had a thought, but this was still a big breakthrough, you'll have to admit.

They also developed new and improved fertilizer and new kinds of plants. They got two, four, six, eight times as much crop from every acre. Here's a quote from the '90s: "Defoliants and herbicides have sprung forward as well, nearly eliminating the need for cultivation during the growing season. It also made possible a no-till farming, allowing virtually no field preparation and, therefore, reduced its soil erosion, planting time, and labor cost. There are now virtually no crop losses from insects such as a boll weevil, corn borer, and Army worm."[20]

Consolidation made for a much prettier countryside. I love all the endless fields of soybeans, stretching out without any interruption. I love the neat forests, where the trees are perfectly spaced and grow so fast. Those Tyson-Exxon Animalplexes that fill all the spaces between the interstate clusters can really crank out the livestock, with brains and without, and recycle the manure right into their own facilities and use it to grow bok choy, water chestnuts, pomegranates, litchi nuts, papaya, and other popular southern foods. (The big breakthrough came, in my opinion, when they figured out how to make dynamite tofucue.)

Of course, when they started building those giant ag units, and when all the jobs were in the city, something had to go. Scattered among all those inefficient little farms were places they called "towns." Basically, judging from the pictures, it looks like they were primitive interstate clusters without the convenience. They had a few stores—a lot of them not even franchises—and lots of things like antique shops, barbershops, and grocery stores. Some people are just stubborn or lazy.

Anyway, those places began to die off pretty quickly. First, they became outposts of the franchises. Some crummy franchises, those that couldn't make it along the interstates, moved into towns, or to the edge of towns, and people seemed glad to see them. They began to go there for food and groceries and hardware and stuff, kind of practicing for consolidation.

The big watershed there, of course, was Wal-to-Wal Mart, though on these old pictures it looks like it began with just one "wal." People liked being treated just like anybody else. You could go there and buy embarrassing stuff, and nobody would know you or ask why you needed something like that. You didn't have to stop and jaw with somebody your mother knew or whatever. And they were cheap. People always like that. (The worse thing about Wal-Mart was their goofy smiley face logo that appears all over their stuff back at the turn of the century. It's hard to believe people fell for that. They were just simpler back then, not quite as smart as we are, I guess.)

Some people complained about there just being a few kinds of stores repeated over and over on the landscape, but I fail to see what's so great about having to hunt for stuff you want to buy, paying different prices for it, and so on. People can be nostalgic for the darnedest things.

Fortunately, they started figuring out how to have fun back then. People began to build consolidated entertainment, though, of course, they didn't have that word for it then.

As early as 2000, the South was filled with places to go to get real concentrated, guaranteed fun. They have a map here in the archive. There were amusement parks of one kind or another from King's Dominion in Virginia to a sort of country-music heaven in Branson, Missouri. There was Orlando, of course, when it was just a tiny thing compared with the world center of culture it now is, with Disney University and all. And there was Spoleto in Charleston and Mardi Gras in New Orleans, and the great beaches from the Outer Banks all the way around to the Texas Gulf. (It's hard to believe that at one time California's beaches were considered cooler than the South's— not to be confused with merely colder—even before the Quake of 2014.)

But my favorite old-fashioned early-consolidated fun place was in the mountains. It was called Dollywood. "Dolly" was apparently some kind of singer or something, but that doesn't matter. Just listen to their statement of vision off what they called "websites" back then. It's so early consolidationist!

> Vision: Our stated reason for existence is to create memories worth repeating for our customers through quality entertainment and fun delivered by genuinely friendly and caring people in a wholesome family environment where American traditions are openly cherished and delivered with the heartfelt emotions so naturally projected by Dolly herself. . . .
>
> All Unconditionally Guaranteed: Quite simply, that means that every day we stand behind every product, service and personal experience you have at Dollywood and guarantee it to your total satisfaction. Should you be dissatisfied in any way during your visit, contact any Dollywood Host or Hostess in the theme park.[21]

In some ways, we haven't improved on that. It's kind of like the Declaration of Independence, where they sort of nail something the first time.

A place not far from here, Stone Mountain, had some cool ideas. In a great consolidationist move, they built a place to re-create the small-town and farm South that was disappearing every day! And they did it with style. Get this: "The 'four-dimensional' theater will open in 2002 and will show a film about the South, the smell of cornbread filling the arena and mist falling on the audience when it rains on the screen. In 2004, a Reconstruction-era Atlanta main street will be recreated." That was so ahead of its time. (Note to self: Do some research on what "cornbread" is. I'm guessing it was bread somehow made out of corn, but that seems unlikely.)[22]

A lot of the South became a great recreation area, especially once you got rid of those little farms; they made great golf courses, with the quaint ranch houses, satellite dishes, barns, and such as interesting hazards. It was about then, I guess, that golf became the great southern sport. You can play it year-round down here. It's funny that it began with old guys in funny clothes actually driving vehicles on the courses, since today it's the very best athletes who play it. Now that the courses stretch over many miles, and you have to run from hole to hole, it's becoming what it should have been all along.

A lot of people who had left by the millions at the first chance early in the twentieth century began to come back South to see where their black ancestors had lived and where the events of the Great Freedom had been enacted. The South turned out to be great at tourism, and people flocked here from all over the world, as they still do, of course. [23]

It's kind of funny, but just when this consolidation was really taking off some southern people celebrated something that had happened back in the ancient days of the 1800s, the Civil War. To some people, watching the South change so fast—with black people getting political power, and the cities spreading and all—they thought they'd better hold on to what they thought made the South the South. They didn't realize that the South had always changed and always would change and that trying to grab one part of that and call it the real South wasn't going to work.

But I guess these folks just hadn't seen enough of the Consolidation to realize how deep it was going to go, and so they made a big deal out of the Confederate flag and stuff. I never really got into ancient history that much, so I don't understand all that, like how they could want to fly the Confederate flag and the United States flag from the same flagpole, since I thought the point of the Confederacy was to leave the United States. But I guess I missed that day in school or whatever.

For a long time people thought that the South had to be all about that part of ancient history or it wasn't about anything. A lot of their entertainment and tourism and stuff dressed itself up like ancient days. I mean you can still see that, but it's kind of like acting like everybody in England wore armor or whatever. History is happening all the time and it's a shame to waste any of it by just getting caught up in one little part of it—especially the worst part!

I guess that's why the chambers of commerce and stuff finally began to resist those white folks who always wanted to talk about the Confederates and the flags and all. Pretty soon people began to see that they lost more customers than they gained with that. They started building museums and monuments to other southern times, like the Great Freedom. They built entertainment villages that reconstructed life back in the 1960s. They have people reenacting sit-ins and marches, all in authentic outfits that some people spent a lot of time getting just right. That's hard these days, when it's tough to get blue denim anymore after people got so sick of so-called natural fabrics around the turn of the century and replaced it with the synths.

Anyway, while all this was going on during the Great Consolidation, the churches had been doing great. The churches had been really segregated for a long time, but by 1998 "about 70 percent of whites and 60 percent of blacks said they worshipped with people of other races."[24]

Enormous churches began to go up, bigger than Wal-to-Wal Marts. The biggest, of course, was the Southern Baptist Pentecostal Ecumenical Brotherhood, which pulled in all different sorts of people.

But you had all other kinds of combinations, too, with just about all the churches on earth setting up southern outposts.

In fact, the churches were real pioneers in consolidating the South. All those new people flooding into the South, whatever so-called race they were, went into the churches. The churches welcomed them and gave them a warm place to feel at home. The southern churches had always been built around bringing in new members, and all these newcomers were perfect for them.

Here's a quote I should use for the paper. A minister from Tennessee said that "the most innovative idea in merchandising has been the shopping center which enables the customer to park conveniently and have his complete shopping needs satisfied at one location." The church, he argued, should offer as many activities as possible—"buses to bring people to church; nurseries; Sunday school classes for all ages; radio and television programs; publications; the cassette tape ministry; and classes, programs, and counseling for singles, the elderly, the poor, the sick, the imprisoned, and the 'bereaved.'"[25]

The churches began to take over a lot of what the government used to do. If you belonged to the church, you were taken care of. They built their own schools, where they could teach whatever they wanted to, even their own kind of science, and where people could pray at ball games and pep rallies and such as well as in class and at assembly and in between. Those schools got richer and richer, while the schools for people who didn't belong to the church got real weak.

That's when the schools became franchised. Now that the Learn-a-Lot Company competes with the Knowledge-R-Us schools, everything is a lot better. Now, kids who can pass the Standards of Learning tests (which they have to do before they can get married, of course) are turned out like hamburgers at the very best consolidated restaurants. (I'm really glad I'm a Learn-a-Lot kid myself. Our golf teams are a lot better, for one thing.)

The prisons were even easier than the schools to franchise. There had been some whining by dinosaur types about so-called public schools being better than the church or franchised ones, but they whined less about the prisons. Incarceration Incorporated's monthly reports showed their numbers way up, almost steadily. They got people in those prisons and kept them there where they could be improved, ready to live in a consolidated society or at least to stay out of the way.

Gaming really helped pay for what little government was left after the schools and prisons had been franchised. Every state except one or two back in 2000 had gambling in the South. My favorite was South Carolina, where they saw the way to consolidation early on. Here's something from a newspaper article from back in '99: "no state's can compare with South Carolina's video poker operation, and with about 3.8 million people, there are more than 29,600 video poker machines. . . . Video poker games can be found everywhere around the state: in mom-and-pop country stores, service stations, bowling alleys and beauty parlors, and in clusters that are called malls, parlors, palaces or game rooms."[26]

That was so cool, because it was just like franchises: you could have gambling everywhere, all the time, and it was always the same. You didn't have to go out of your way or confront weird stuff.

But the gambling people, of course, made a big mistake. They got tangled up in politics. Or, it appears from these old news shows that I'm scanning, politics got tangled up in gambling.

It wasn't that the gamblers or the politicians were looking for trouble. They knew they had it good, and they didn't want to rock the boat.

A lot of people wanted the government to "get out of the way," as they put it. (Note to self: Did they also want to get rid of themselves, or just other people in the government? That's not clear from the speeches and stuff I see here.)

A lot of the people moving to the South back around '00 were retired, back when people worked as hard as they could for their whole lives and then suddenly stopped, as unlikely as that sounds.

Those retired folks were generally pretty well off. They had savings, and they owned their own houses. But they had already raised their kids, and they didn't much like being taxed to educate other people's kids and take care of poor people and such. They thought the churches and franchises could do that better than the government.

So then came the biggest political event of the Consolidated South: the Gambling Alliance. Dr. John Roulette formed the party in 2034, with the backing of a lot people. His idea was simple: Abolish taxes and let the government pay for itself with the proceeds from gambling. Follow the South Carolina model and put not only video poker but every other kind of game in every nook and cranny. Keep them running all the time. Follow the Mississippi model and put up casinos in the abandoned farmland outside of cities. Get outsiders to come in and pay to play on the machines.

A lot of people loved the idea, and Roulette won the governorship of the Consolidated South. Dr. Roulette was very persuasive, especially with all those ads.

But we all know what happened. It turns out that gambling wasn't that firm a foundation for even the little bit of government that was left. A lot of people who had gambled the most ran out of money—even the older folks lost their houses. They started hanging around the edges of the agricultural units, and some people even tried growing their own food. Some really desperate people set up their own little "businesses," selling stuff themselves without the approval of the franchises. Some people taught their children themselves or let them go without schooling altogether. Incarceration Incorporated had almost more work than they could handle, tracking people down and sending them off.

Governor Roulette cracked down as much as he could, but, ironically, he didn't have enough power left to get things under control. He had to turn to Wal-to-Wal Mart and Tyson-Exxon and even Knowledge-R-Us to restore order. After the Seven Bad Years they kind of got things back under control.

Some people say that we'll never get out of debt and that there are just too many Incarceration Incorporated officers everywhere, but I remain hopeful. I have my whole life in front of me. After all, I know that the South, back in the ancient days, went through hard times before. "Tomorrow is another day"—that's the motto of the Consolidated South. And tomorrow I have to turn these notes into a presentation, so I guess I'd better get to sleep. Night.

NOTES
I would like to thank Scott Matthews for his research assistance and advice for this essay.

1. *The State of the South, 2000* (Chapel Hill: MDC, September 2000), 49.
2. *Atlanta Journal-Constitution*, July 23, 1998.
3. *Christian Science Monitor*, July 28, 2000.
4. *State of the South*, 6.
5. *State of the South*, 13–14.
6. *Charlottesville Daily Progress*, October 3, 2000.
7. *Christian Science Monitor*, June 10, 2000.
8. *State of the South*, 39.

9. *USA Today*, October 20, 2000.

10. *Smart Growth in the Southeast: New Approaches for Guiding Development* (Charlottesville: Southern Environmental Law Center, 1999), 3.

11. *Smart Growth*, 4.

12. *Smart Growth*, 4.

13. Andy Serwer, "Ground Zero: Capital of the Net? The tech boom has changed Washington's balance of power. Guess who's winning . . . ," *Fortune*, October 9, 2000, 240, 248.

14. *Atlanta Journal-Constitution*, January 18, 1998.

15. *Atlanta Journal-Constitution*, November 12, 1999.

16. *Wall Street Journal*, March 6, 1998.

17. *Atlanta Journal-Constitution*, July 4, 2000.

18. R. Douglas Hurt, ed., *The Rural South since World War II* (Baton Rouge: Louisiana State University Press, 1998), 2.

19. Hurt, *Rural South*, 18–21.

20. Hurt, *Rural South*, 21–27.

21. *Our Company Culture*, Dollywood Company, October 2000 <http://www.dollywood.com/Gen_Mission.htm>.

22. *New York Times*, October 8, 2000.

23. *New York Times*, March 1, 1993.

24. *Atlanta Journal-Constitution*, July 23, 1998.

25. Ted Ownby, "Struggling to Be Old-Fashioned," in Hurt, *Rural South*, 126. The first quotation is from the minister; the list of activities is from Ownby.

26. *Washington Post*, February 1999.

Contributors

EDWARD L. AYERS is the Hugh P. Kelly Professor of History and the Dean of Arts and Sciences at the University of Virginia. He is the author of *Vengeance and Justice: Crime and Punishment in the Nineteenth-Century American South* (1984), *The Promise of the New South: Life after Reconstruction* (1992)(a finalist for both the National Book Award and the Pulitzer Prize), coeditor of *The Oxford Book of the American South* (1997), and coauthor of *All Over the Map: Rethinking American Regions* (1996). Ayers's current work is "The Valley of the Shadow: Two Communities in the American Civil War."

THADIOUS M. DAVIS is Gertrude Conaway Vanderbilt Professor of English at Vanderbilt University. She is the author of the biography, *Nella Larsen, Novelist of the Harlem Renaissance* (1994), and of

Faulkner's "Negro": Art and the Southern Context (1983). Her most recent book, *Games of Property: Race, Gender, Law, and Faulkner's "Go Down Moses"* (Duke University Press, 2002), marks a return to Faulkner studies.

FRED HOBSON is Lineberger Professor in the Humanities and coeditor of the *Southern Literary Journal* at the University of North Carolina at Chapel Hill. A contributor to the *Atlantic Monthly*, the *New York Times Book Review*, and other publications, he is the author, most recently, of *Mencken: A Life* (Random House, 1994) and *But Now I See: The White Southern Racial Conversion Narrative* (LSU Press, 1999).

LINDA WAGNER-MARTIN is Frank Borden Hanes Professor of English at University of North Carolina at Chapel Hill. Her recent books include *Sylvia Plath, A Literary Life* (1999); *Historical Guide to Ernest Hemingway* (2000); and The Bedford Cultural Studies Edition of Gertrude Stein's *Three Lives* (2000). She writes regularly on the American modernists—Faulkner, Hemingway, Dos Passos, William Carlos Williams, Stein, and others.

JOEL WILLIAMSON is Lineberger Professor in the Humanities (emeritus) at the University of North Carolina at Chapel Hill. He has published work on black-white relations in the South, most notably in *New People* (1980) and *The Crucible of Race* (1984). In 1993 he published *William Faulkner and Southern History*, a study designed to place the author and his work in the context of southern culture. He is now at work on a book to be entitled "The Feminine Elvis."